ABOUT THE AUTHORS

Jenny Hyson is the Children's Adviser for the Oxford diocese and author. In her role as diocesan adviser, Jenny is well known for the creative material she produces for training and worship with children in mind. Her work also includes the important areas of Child Protection and Children and Holy Communion, and she is an enthusiastic accredited trainer for *Godly Play*.

Canon David Winter is a writer and broadcaster. He is also Consulting Editor to the *People's Bible Commentary* series and has written a number of books for BRF including *After the Gospels*, *With Jesus in the Upper Room* and *Hope in the Wilderness*.

Text copyright © Jenny Hyson and David Winter 2004
Illustrations copyright © Mary Hall 2004
The authors assert the moral right
to be identified as the authors of this work

Published by
The Bible Reading Fellowship
First Floor, Elsfield Hall
15–17 Elsfield Way, Oxford OX2 8FG

ISBN 1 84101 306 4
First published 2004
10 9 8 7 6 5 4 3 2 1 0
All rights reserved

Acknowledgments
Unless otherwise stated, scripture quotations are taken from the Contemporary English Version of the Bible published by HarperCollins Publishers, copyright © 1991, 1992, 1995 American Bible Society.

Scripture quotations from The New Revised Standard Version of the Bible, Anglicized Edition, copyright © 1989, 1995 by the Division of Christian Education of the National Council of the Churches of Christ in the United States of America, are used by permission. All rights reserved.

A catalogue record for this book is available from the British Library

Printed and bound in Malta

SHARING LIFE THROUGH ADVENT

IDEAS FOR THE ADVENT JOURNEY FOR CHURCH, HOME
AND COLLECTIVE WORSHIP BASED ON THE THREE-YEAR LECTIONARY

Jenny Hyson with David Winter

CONTENTS

Foreword 6
Introduction 7

YEAR A: PILGRIMAGE

Sharing life through worship 10
Sharing life through Advent with children 14
Sharing life through Advent with families 22
Sharing life through Advent Bible reading notes 31
Sharing life through collective worship 35

YEAR B: PROMISES

Sharing life through worship 42
Sharing life through Advent with children 45
Sharing life through Advent with families 55
Sharing life through Advent Bible reading notes 64
Sharing life through collective worship 68

YEAR C: COMING

Sharing life through worship 76
Sharing life through Advent with children 80
Sharing life through Advent with families 89
Sharing life through Advent Bible reading notes 98
Sharing life through collective worship 102

FOREWORD

Ministry alongside children is one of the most complex, demanding and important ministries in the Church. Children bring with them a wonderful diversity of experience, understanding and response, and when we share our faith with them, it has to be more than just imparting information. We have to share something of ourselves. Too frequently this precious ministry has been marginalized by congregations and seen as secondary to the main life of the Church as expressed in the Sunday liturgy. This has led to a disconnection between the teaching and preaching offered to adults and that which is shared with the children.

The temptation is ever there to approach this ministry by 'thinking of something to do' with the children on a Sunday morning, rather than reflecting on what we can share with them as we worship through the seasons of the Christian calendar. Giving in to this temptation can lead to the impression that faith is simply about knowing Bible stories and, as we know only too well, impressions formed in childhood stay with us.

Jenny Hyson and David Winter offer us a valuable opportunity to enrich our ministry during Advent—not just with children but with the whole congregation. *Sharing Life through Advent* addresses the issues outlined above by providing ideas and resources that enliven our use of the lectionary during this season. Rooting this material in the Common Lectionary enables a link between a liturgy of the word for adults and a sharing of the word with children. The way in which the scripture is addressed can be differentiated by age, needs and experience but is held together creatively in a shared approach.

This book encourages further opportunities for sharing by offering ways in which the whole congregation can engage in this Advent season of preparation. As is so often the case, when we address the needs of young people in our church, we discover ways in which we can encourage adults as well. By describing how these themes can also be used within the family or in collective worship in school, the possibilities for engaging imaginatively with the Sunday lectionary are taken beyond the confines of church and into the norms and daily rhythms of children's lives.

This book leaves plenty of room for imagination and interpretation but marks out an attractive pathway to lead all ages to worship together at the manger, sharing life as children of the same heavenly Father.

The Rt Revd David Rossdale, the Bishop of Grimsby

INTRODUCTION

Sharing Life through Advent is a combined resource for use in worship, children's groups, in the home or in school during collective worship. The material is written for church and children's leaders, adults, parents and children, and can be used by large or small groups, on a Sunday or midweek. The readings for each of the sessions follow the Common Lectionary readings for the four weeks of Advent, as set for years A, B and C. Within each year you will find ideas for sharing Advent in the following areas of life.

SHARING LIFE THROUGH WORSHIP

Included in the worship material are ideas for making the lighting of the Advent candle an integral part of the whole service. Each of the three years offers a different approach to the liturgy and can be used for adult worship or if children are present.

SHARING LIFE THROUGH ADVENT WITH CHILDREN

This section offers material for twelve sessions over the three years, with suggestions for storytelling, activities, wondering questions, craft ideas and candle prayer times.

SHARING LIFE THROUGH ADVENT WITH FAMILIES

This section offers activities, discussion starters and Christmas craft ideas for use by families during Advent. The material stands on its own or builds on the material used on a Sunday in worship or children's groups.

SHARING LIFE THROUGH ADVENT BIBLE READING NOTES

In order to help adults reflect more deeply on the material, special notes have been provided to give deeper insight into the relevant Bible passages for each week of Advent in the three years. These notes may be photocopied and used by adult members of the congregation, whether or not they are also using the family material.

SHARING LIFE THROUGH COLLECTIVE WORSHIP

This section provides ideas for short acts of collective worship with children in Key Stages 1 and 2. The material builds on the ideas already available in the 'Sharing life through Advent with children' section, which can be supplemented into the collective worship material depending on the situation and number of children present.

The resource follows three different themes over the three years, allowing for a new perspective each year.

Year A   Pilgrimage
Year B   Promises
Year C   Coming

Each Advent ends its journey kneeling at the foot of the manger, where once more the reader can wonder at the mystery of the Christ-child, come to earth to dwell among us.

> *The Word became a human being and lived here with us. We saw his true glory, the glory of the only Son of the Father. From him all the kindness and all the truth of God have come down to us.*
> JOHN 1:14

★★★ YEAR A ★★★

PILGRIMAGE

SHARING LIFE THROUGH WORSHIP

INTRODUCTION

It is hoped that members of the congregation will be encouraged to use the Bible reading notes and prayers for adults and the 'Sharing life through Advent with families' material as part of their ongoing worship throughout Advent. An Advent candle may also be purchased and used as a simple focal point for worship.

Advent is a time of waiting and anticipation for the coming of the promised Messiah. The project follows the Isaiah readings as set in the Lectionary for Advent. The first three readings encourage that sense of preparing and waiting for the time when 'all things will be made new'. Advent Four invites us to celebrate the coming Messiah, as described in the reading from Luke. But we are also challenged to look deeper into what Isaiah is calling us to share in—the challenge of journeying together towards the ultimate goal, God's peaceful city of Zion.

The material in this section offers ideas and liturgical responses for use during the lighting of the Advent candles. The timing of the lighting of the candles may differ according to local situations. The material can be used either by an adult congregation or with an all-age congregation. The Bible reading notes might equally be used in home groups.

LIGHTING THE ADVENT CANDLES DURING SUNDAY WORSHIP

If the children are present at the beginning of the service, they could share in the lighting of the Advent candle. After this they might go off into their groups during the singing of an appropriate hymn to use the children's material. If, however, the children come in towards the end of the service, the lighting of the Advent candles may be kept until they are present. The children could then be invited to share their reflections by way of an introduction to the reading. Following the lighting of the Advent candle, members of the congregation could be encouraged to take the light out with them into the rest of the week by using the candle and materials offered in the family section (see page 22).

The suggested pattern for each week is as follows:

- The introduction given in the liturgical notes is read.
- Where appropriate, a few simple open questions might be asked.
- The Old Testament reading is read by a member of the congregation.
- At the end of the reading, allow a few moments for quiet reflection.
- A child or young person might be invited to light the Advent candle or candles.
- The prayer given in the liturgical notes is then said either by the young person or the whole congregation.

SHARING LIFE THROUGH ADVENT WITH THE WHOLE CONGREGATION

Choose four points in the church where a focus for each Sunday of Advent can be staged. This might include a suitable flower arrangement, focal objects, Advent candle and drapes. Different groups in the congregation might take responsibility for looking at the text for a particular Sunday, and then designing a focal area that will complement the Bible story. You could encourage church flower arrangers to be part of the project. Each focal area will need to include a candle.

There are two options for the use of these areas within the service:

- Each Sunday of Advent the congregation could be invited to turn to face the week's focal point. In smaller congregations or where space allows, the congregation could be encouraged to gather around the focus. Each week a new focus area is developed,

and each new candle is lit by carrying the light from the first Advent candle. By week 4, candles one, two and three will all be lit first, giving a sense of journeying and moving forward to the lighting of the fourth candle.
- Where an Advent wreath is traditionally placed at the front of the church, a candle may be lit in the focal area for the reading and reflection, and then carried forward either to be placed in the Advent wreath or to light the appropriate candle there. (For instruction on how to make an Advent wreath, see page 80.)

SUGGESTIONS FOR THE FOUR FOCAL POINTS

Advent 1: Pilgrimage to Jerusalem

ISAIAH 2:1–5

Position this week's focus near the aisle or close to the church door. The church door is the point at which certain journeys begin: the aisle is used for processions, weddings, walking to receive Holy Communion and as a focal point for funerals.

The focus might include:

- Suitable drapes and flowers arranged to give the sense of movement.
- A gold flower arrangement, or similar, towards the top (symbolic of the glory of Zion, the holy city—the goal of our journeying).
- Pictures of war (maybe taken from newspapers or downloaded from the internet), standing alongside farming tools.
- Sheets of foil alongside a hammer.
- The first of the Advent candles.

Advent 2: The peaceful kingdom

ISAIAH 11:1–10

The position for this week's focus could be the font as the reading speaks of new beginnings, symbolic in baptism. In churches where a font is not permanently placed, the font might be positioned and incorporated into the focus.

The focus might include:

- A branch from a tree interlaced with an appropriately coloured drape, maybe rising to the font, and a white flower arrangement. White is a symbol of purity and characteristic of the Messiah's style of judgment and rule.
- A pair of scales, to symbolize the idea of judgment.
- The second of the Advent candles.

Advent 3: God's sacred highway

ISAIAH 35:1–10

Position this week's focus at the lectern, the point from which the word of the Lord is proclaimed.

The focus might include the following:

- Drapes in desert colours, used as a backdrop to a series of smaller flower arrangements.
- A dish or jug of water—better still, a small indoor bubble pool made by placing a small fishtank pump in an earthenware pot.
- Cover the pump with pebbles and add enough water to give a bubbling effect when plugged in. Finish the pot by adding tall grasses or reeds around the edge.
- The third Advent candle.

Advent 4: The new king is coming

LUKE 1:26–38

The position of this week's focus could be the pulpit—again, a point at which God's word is announced. In those churches where there isn't a pulpit, the focus could be placed at the front of the church on the opposite side to the focus for Advent 3.

The focus might include:

- Drapes in blue and white, the colours traditionally associated with Mary.
- Two flower arrangements, each a different single colour. One arrangement might be yellow and gold for the angel; and the second white, symbolic of Mary's virginity. Place one arrangement higher than the other, with light sprays of flowers from each touching in the centre. This could symbolize Mary's simple acceptance of the angel's message.
- The fourth Advent candle.

Once each focus has been set up, it can remain in place

for the remaining weeks of Advent. For example, on the third Sunday of Advent the displays for Advent 1 and 2 will remain in place and the focus for Advent 3 will be introduced for the first time. This will give a sense of continuity and journeying from one to the other as well as anticipation for the next week.

CHRISTMAS DAY

On Christmas Day, the focus will of course be the nativity, placed at the centre of the four displays. The nativity draws together the threads of the Advent journey, celebrating the birth of the Messiah as prophesied by Isaiah; but the light of Christ still shines on in the darkness beyond Christmas and, as the final Advent candle is lit, we can pause and look back on the journey so far—to all that has been fulfilled. Then, in faith and hope we can turn to face the road ahead, ready to continue on the journey, sharing life together while all the time pressing forward towards the peaceful city of Zion and the fulfilment of all that is yet to come.

SUGGESTIONS FOR ADVENT LITURGY

ADVENT 1

Introductory sentence

'Let us go up the hill of the Lord, to the temple of Israel's God.'

Reading

ISAIAH 2:1–5

The prophet foresees a time when every nation will turn to the true God, turning from their ancient hatreds and learning to live together in peace.

After the reading, light the Advent candle.

Prayers

Lord Jesus, light of the world, born in David's city of Bethlehem, born like David to be a king, be born in our hearts this Christmastide. Be king of our lives today.

God of hope, give us this Advent a faith that looks inwards to the deepest longings of our own hearts, upwards to the heavenly city and out to the whole world. Hold before our eyes your vision of hope as we wait joyfully for the coming of the Saviour. Amen

ADVENT 2

Introductory sentence

'The land will be as full of knowledge of the Lord as the seas are full of water.'

Reading

ISAIAH 11:1–10

From a descendant of David, God will bring blessing to the whole world.

After the reading, light the Advent candle.

Prayers

Lord Jesus, light of the world, the prophets ordained that you would bring peace and save your people in trouble. Give peace in our hearts this Christmastide and show all the world God's love.

Lord God of creation, we long to see the whole world renewed and want to play our part in your vision of recreation. Renew us by your life-giving Spirit, so that we can be agents of your peace and justice in the world and be part of your great purpose for the whole of creation.

ADVENT 3

Introductory sentence

> *'The desert will rejoice and flowers will bloom in the wilderness.'*

Reading

ISAIAH 35:1–10

God's sacred highway leads to the place of joy and gladness.
   After the reading, light the Advent candle.

Prayers

Lord Jesus, light of the world, John the Baptist told the people to prepare, for you were very near. Help us to be ready to welcome you now.

God of mercy and love, set us free from the old way, the desert way, and bring us on to that sacred highway of holiness, which leads to you.

ADVENT 4

Introductory sentence

> *'I am the Lord's servant. Let it happen as you have said.'*

Reading

LUKE 1:26–38

The angel Gabriel tells Mary that she will be the mother of Jesus, the Son of God Most High.
   After the reading, light the Advent candle.

Prayers

Lord Jesus, light of the world, blessed in Gabriel who brought good news, blessed in Mary your mother, bless your Church preparing for Christmas, and bless us your children who long for your coming.

Grant to us, like Mary, a faith that takes you at your word and in simple obedience seeks to do your will. Amen

SHARING LIFE THROUGH ADVENT WITH CHILDREN

INTRODUCTION

There was a time, way back at the very beginning, when everything in God's world was perfect. The story tells how the first people, named Adam and Eve, lived happily with each other and with God. God wanted to be friends with his people but it wasn't long before they wanted to do things their own way, even if that meant hurting God and others. They no longer cared about God. Although the people turned away from God, still God loved them and tried all kinds of ways to show them his love.

Things haven't really changed today. People still care more about themselves than they do about God and others, and the results lead to unhappiness, quarrelling in families and between friends, bullying and stealing from one another and fighting between different countries.

Now there was, in those early days, a man called Abraham. Abraham and his family loved and trusted God, so God talked to Abraham and promised him that he would make him the father of a great and special nation called Israel.

As time went on, God tried to show the people of Israel how to live happily together by giving them the ten best ways to live. We know these ten best ways as the Ten Commandments. However, it soon became clear that the people of Israel found the Ten Commandments too hard to keep. No matter how many times God forgave the people, still they forgot about the ten best ways to live.

But God did not forget his people, Israel, or the promises he gave to them. God gave them good kings to rule over them, kings like David who loved God and followed his laws—but still the people chose to do things their own way. God saw that he would need to send a very special king.

To prepare the way, God sent many messengers, called prophets, to tell the people about this special king, who they called the Messiah. He would show them a new way to live. One of these special messengers was called Isaiah and he began to tell the people what this new king would be like.

Advent is one of the Church's special seasons when we get ready and wait to celebrate again the birth of that special king—God's very own son, Jesus. So, through Advent, we will look at what the prophet Isaiah told the people their new king would be like, and we will begin to see how God kept his promise. But the prophet Isaiah also has a message for us today. He invites us, as if we are on a journey, to work towards a time when there will be no more wars, no more fighting, no more unfairness, no more pain. We are invited to join with others, as if on a pilgrimage, to see how God wants us to live and how to prepare for the time when Jesus will come again and all things will finally be made new.

During this Advent, take time out to listen to what Isaiah had to say and think about what God might want you to do to get ready for that special day.

SUGGESTIONS FOR MAKING A SPECIAL FOCAL POINT

- Create a special focus point in your room during Advent where you can place the candle, ready for the children to arrive. You might like to place it on a purple cloth, as the liturgical colour for Advent is purple.

✶

ADVENT 1: PILGRIMAGE TO JERUSALEM

ISAIAH 2:1–5

SETTING THE SCENE

Jerusalem was the capital city of the people of Israel and it was here that the people of Israel built their first temple, where they could worship God. For thousands of years, people from all different countries travelled to Jerusalem. Some people went just to visit the city, but many travelled there on a pilgrimage. A pilgrimage is a special journey that people take to visit a sacred place where they can worship. Today Jerusalem is still an important place for Jews, Christians and Muslims. In the centre of Jerusalem there are many churches and a beautiful mosque with a golden dome. It is a place that many people still go on pilgrimage to, from all over the world.

WONDERING

- I wonder if you have ever been on a long journey to somewhere special?
- What kind of things did you need to take with you?

Tell the children that you are going to take them on an imaginary journey and that you want them to take something with them. Give each of the children a piece of silver foil and tell them to put it on the floor in front of them. Now invite the children to sit very still and to close their eyes. Encourage them to use their imaginations as you begin to paint a picture in words.

'Imagine you are on a special journey and on the way you begin to meet up with people from all kinds of different places. You notice that they are wearing different clothes than you, and some of them are speaking in different languages. But as you walk along, you realize that you all seem to be going to the same place.'

Read Isaiah 2:1–2.

'Imagine your first glimpse of this special place. It is still a long way off but you can see it towering above all the other mountains.

- I wonder what it looks like?
- I wonder how you feel?

'People around you begin to talk to one another, saying, "Let's go to the mountain of the Lord God of Jacob and worship in his temple. The Lord will teach us his Law from Jerusalem, and we will obey him."

'You keep moving forward, climbing up the steep hill. It's hard work but before long you reach the top.

'Look around. How do you feel now that you have arrived at your destination?'

Pause for a few moments and then invite the children to open their eyes and to share their responses. After the responses, ask the children to take their piece of silver foil and to fold and shape it carefully into a sword. Tell the children to try not to tear the foil.

Now read Isaiah 2:3b–4. What happened when God spoke to the people?

This time invite the children to take their silver foil sword and flatten it out, then to reshape it into a useful tool.

'On this first Sunday of Advent, Isaiah points to a day when people from all nations will come together to listen to God. But we know that even when God sent his very own son, Jesus, into the world, still the people did not listen. Jesus promised that one day he would come again and at that time nations would never again go to war, never prepare for battle again. This Advent, we can remember when Jesus first came to earth just as the prophet Isaiah said he would, and we can look forward to when Jesus will come again.'

PICTURING THE BIBLE

Read Isaiah 2:1–5 and talk about what the writer is saying. You might like to use some of these reflection pointers to help with the discussion.

- I wonder who the people in the story are?
- I wonder what they might be saying to each other?
- I wonder what picture you would paint about this story?
- I wonder where this place really is?
- I wonder which part of the story you like the best?

CANDLE TIME

Invite the children into a circle. Place the candle where everyone can see, then light the candle. Pause for a few moments and let the children look at the candle. Invite the children to reflect again on what Isaiah said. (You might want to use similar questions to those used at the beginning of the session.)

Now invite the children to think about a world with no more fighting—a world where there are no more arguments and where people are kind to one another.

Think about how the people in today's reading went on a journey, how they asked God to show them how to make the world a better place. Invite the children to think about how they too can help to make the world a better place today, perhaps by being kind and caring for one another.

PRAYER FOR THE WEEK

Heavenly Father, help us to make the world a better place by being kind and thoughtful to one another. Amen

CRAFT ACTIVITY

Take a long piece of frieze paper or lining wallpaper. Draw or paint the outline of the road leading to Jerusalem. Invite the children to draw themselves on the road to Jerusalem. Stick on to the picture the foil swords now changed into useful tools.

If time is limited, the background could already be prepared and the children could draw pictures of themselves on to pieces of paper, which could then be cut out and stuck on to the picture.

At the top of the paper, write the words from Isaiah 2:3: 'Let's go to the mountain of the Lord. He will teach us his Law.'

✴

ADVENT 2: THE PEACEFUL KINGDOM

ISAIAH 11:1–10

SETTING THE SCENE

In the reading for the second Sunday of Advent, the prophet Isaiah tells us that the 'new king', often called the 'Messiah', will be a descendant of King David. Remind the children that King David was one of the good kings that God chose to reign over the people of Israel.

PICTURING THE BIBLE

Read Isaiah 11:1–10 and talk about what the writer is saying. You might like to use some of the reflection pointers to help with the discussion.

- I wonder what picture you would paint about this story?
- I wonder what the story is saying to us?
- I wonder which is your favourite part of the story?
- I wonder if today's reading gives us any clues about Jesus?

WONDERING

Ask the children to imagine what it would be like if they were put in charge of a country. What would they want to see happen? What changes would they like to make? Write the children's answers on a large sheet of paper. Now look at what the prophet Isaiah said the new king would be like.

Read Isaiah 11:2–5 and 10. On small cards, have written the key words from the passage: wisdom, skill to rule, judge fairly, insight, fairness, honesty/integrity, honour, obedient, powerful. How many words in the passage match up with what the children have put on their list? Match up the words by placing the cards alongside those the children have written. The children may have articulated the ideas differently, so you may need to explain the meaning of some of the words to help them to make the connections.

Now ask the children how they decide the difference between what is right and what is wrong. Talk about what might be fair and unfair punishment.

While the children continue to reflect on this, read the second half of the Isaiah passage, Isaiah 11:6–9.

A beautiful picture in words

Isaiah goes on to paint a beautiful picture in words, telling us about a world that is full of peace, but...

- 'I wonder which bit of this peaceful world you would have included?
- 'I wonder if there is anything else that you would like to include in this peaceful world?'

Allow the children time to respond, and then ask them if they noticed what Isaiah said about children: 'Leopards will lie down with young goats, and wolves will rest with lambs. Calves and lions will eat together and be cared for by little children' (v. 6). (Some translations say, 'Little children will lead them.')

- 'I wonder how that makes you feel?'

CANDLE TIME

Invite the children into a circle and place the Advent candle in the centre of the circle. Pause for a few moments and then remind the children that we don't have to wait for a time in the future when the world will be full of peace—we can start to make it happen today. We also don't have to wait until we are grown up, because Isaiah reminds us how important God thinks children are—even little children.

The dove is often used as a symbol of peace. Pass a basket round containing cut-out dove shapes and invite the children to take one each. Now invite the children to think about ways they could start to be a 'peacemaker'. When the children have shared their ideas, light the Advent candle and pray the prayer below, inserting each of the children's and leader's names at the appropriate place.

PRAYER FOR THE WEEK

Dear Lord, please help...(insert names)... to be a peacemaker at home, at school, at work and in the world, so that with your help, we can begin to work towards making the world a more beautiful and peaceful place. Amen

CRAFT ACTIVITY

Turn the children's dove shapes into badges or pendants to show that they are being peacemakers. Ideally the doves should be cut out of thin white card for this activity. For badges, fasten a safety-pin on the back of the shape with tape, or attach the shape to a round ready-made badge shape. For a pendant, punch a hole in the dove shape and thread a piece of ribbon through the hole. Tie a knot in the ribbon.

Alternatively, doves could be given a sprinkling of glitter so that they could be hung up on the Christmas tree.

✱

ADVENT 3: GOD'S SACRED HIGHWAY

ISAIAH 35:1–10

WONDERING

If you can see trees out of the window, take the children to the window and look at the bare trees with no leaves on them. If you cannot see trees, then show the children pictures of trees in winter and trees in spring. Talk about how, in spring, the trees that look dead in the winter will come to life again, growing new leaves. Look together at a flower bulb and talk about how it will be 'transformed' when it is planted in the ground, cared for and allowed to grow.

Now ask the children to imagine what it is like in the desert where there is mile upon mile of sand and no water. Talk about those countries where there is little or no rain, where there is no running water to drink and no rain to help the crops grow. Invite the children to think about what it would be like to live in a country like that.

- I wonder what it's really like in the desert?
- I wonder what it's like to be really thirsty?
- I wonder what it's like to be lost in the desert?
- I wonder what it's like to be found?
- I wonder what it is like to come across an oasis in the desert? (You may need to explain what an oasis is.)

SETTING THE SCENE

In scripture, the words 'desert' or 'wilderness' are used to describe not only the barren deserts of sand dunes or rocks and mountains, but also scrubland or wild pasture suitable for grazing sheep and goats. Often the grass would be burnt up by the summer droughts. The land would be host to wild animals who would seek out their food.

The desert could be a dangerous place, with hot blinding sun by day and freezing cold by night, and yet the desert plays an important part in Bible stories. The Israelites spent many years wandering in the desert, led by God from slavery to freedom. The desert is also symbolic of the struggle between good and bad, right and wrong, trusting in God and turning away from God. Not surprisingly, then, Isaiah uses the image of the desert to show the way the world will be transformed when the new king—the Messiah—comes, and God will ultimately lead his faithful people to safety.

Invite the children to remember how, last week, the prophet Isaiah told us that things in the world would be different when the Messiah came. In today's reading the prophet Isaiah tells of something else that will be changed.

Read Isaiah 35:1–2a and 6b–7. Isaiah talks about a time when the desert will come to life, where the fields will be made fertile and grow all kinds of things, and the dry lands will flow with water. Everything will be transformed.

But that is not all that Isaiah said would happen. Read Isaiah 35:5–6a: 'The blind will see, and the ears of the deaf will be healed. Those who were lame will leap around like deer; tongues once silent will begin to shout.' If we look at some of the stories about Jesus we can see how he began to fulfil what Isaiah said about God's special king.

PICTURING THE BIBLE

Read again Isaiah 35:1–10 and talk about what the writer is saying. You might like to use some of the reflection pointers to help with the discussion.

- I wonder what the story is showing us?
- I wonder which part of the story you like the best?
- I wonder what it would be like if there were no fish in the sea, no birds in the air, or animals in the fields?
- I wonder what you would like to see changed (transformed) or made better in the world today?
- I wonder how we can really care for our world and make a difference?

CRAFT ACTIVITY 1

For this activity you will need enough Bibles for children to have one each or one per group. Have prepared some leaf shapes with the following Bible references written on them. Punch a hole at the bottom of each leaf shape.

- Matthew 9:27–30a
- Matthew 8:1–3
- Matthew 11:2–6
- Luke 4:40
- Matthew 15:29–31
- Luke 17:11–16

Divide the leaves among the children. With larger numbers of children, repeat the verses on different leaf shapes. Invite the children to find the passages in the Bible. When everyone has found their passage, bring the children back into a circle and lead straight in to candle time.

CANDLE TIME

Place a bare twig in a vase in the centre of the circle and invite the children, one by one, to read out the passage they have found showing how Jesus fulfilled Isaiah's prophecy. As the passage is read, ask the child to hang their leaf shape on to the twig, thus transforming it and bringing it to life.

Explain to the children that we are all very special to God. He cares for us, regardless of age, wealth or poverty, or whether we are male or female. Jesus said that if people wanted to be like him, they must show the same kind of love to others as he showed. Being kind to someone can really transform their day, turning sadness into happiness. Christians also believe that God made the world and gave it to us to care for. It is important that we are careful about the way we treat the world around us if we don't want to see it being destroyed by greed and selfishness.

Read again Isaiah 35:8–10. God promises to take care of all those who listen to him and follow his ways and that a time will come when there will be no more sadness.

In a basket already prepared, have enough different coloured flower shapes for the children to choose one each. (Each flower shape should have a hole punched in it.) Pass the basket around and invite each of the children to take a different coloured flower shape. In their own time, invite the children to hang their flower shape on to the twig to show that they want to help to transform God's world today by being kind to others and by caring for God's world.

When all the children are sitting back in the circle, light the Advent candle and place it where everyone can see it. Pause for a few minutes to let the children reflect on the candle.

PRAYER FOR THE WEEK

Hold hands in the circle and pray:

Dear Lord Jesus, help us all to care for your world and each other in the ways that you showed us, so that we can help to make your world a more beautiful place.

CRAFT ACTIVITY 2

You will need:
- Enough lengths of card to make a crown for each child
- Extra leaf shapes cut from the leaf template
- Scissors
- Crayons
- Glue
- Double-sided sticky tape

Cut the length of card to the right length to go round the child's head. Cut out and colour some leaf shapes from the template. Lay the card flat and decorate with the coloured leaves. Place a piece of double-sided sticky tape along one of the short edges of the crown. Measure the crown on the child's head and finish the crown by sticking at the appropriate place.

ADVENT 4: THE NEW KING IS COMING

LUKE 1:26–38

WONDERING

Ask the children if they have ever had to wait a long time for something exciting to happen. It might have been a birthday, a holiday or some other special event. I wonder how it felt having to wait, and then how it felt when the waiting was over? It may seem a long time just waiting for Christmas Day to come, but think how much longer the people of Israel had to wait for the Messiah, the new king that God promised to send.

Ask the children to imagine how the people of Israel might have felt and how they thought the Messiah, the new king of Israel, would come to them. How were they to recognize this special person?

SETTING THE SCENE

Mary was just an ordinary teenager who lived in Nazareth. In those days, people got married at a much younger age than we do today. Mary was engaged to Joseph, a carpenter in the town, who Luke tells us was a descendant of King David.

An angel appeared to Mary and told her that she was to have God's very own son—the long-awaited new king, the Messiah. Isaiah had foretold the birth of God's new king many, many years before: 'But the Lord will still give you proof. A virgin is pregnant; she will have a son and will name him Immanuel' (Isaiah 7:14).

There was nothing special about Mary or Joseph. They weren't royalty, they weren't even famous and yet God chose them to be the parents of his son. I wonder why?

PICTURING THE BIBLE

Read Luke 1:26–38 and talk about the story. You might like to use the reflection pointers to help with the discussion.

- I wonder what Mary was really thinking as she listened to the angel?
- I wonder how Mary was feeling?
- I wonder what angels really look like?
- I wonder if there are angels today?
- I wonder how you might feel if an angel visited you?
- I wonder what picture you would paint about this story?

Begin to draw out the comparison between how the children thought that God's new king might have come and what actually happened. Invite the children to remember how the angel came to Mary to tell her that she was to be the mother of the promised Messiah.

Have available a book that tells the meaning behind different names. (It may be possible to borrow one from a library.) Ask the children if they know why their parents chose their particular name. Now, look in the book and tell each of the children the meaning behind each of their names. If there are a large number of children, you might have looked the names up earlier and written the meanings on pieces of paper to give to each of the children.

When the angel came to tell Mary that she was going to have a special baby, she was told to give the baby the name Jesus. Jesus was a fairly ordinary name but, like most names, it has a meaning. The name Jesus means 'rescuer'. The story in the Bible tells us that Mary was worried about what the angel was telling her, but look again at what Mary replied: 'I am the Lord's servant! Let it happen as you have said.'

Mary said 'yes' to God. She trusted the angel's message and she trusted God, even though maybe she still felt scared. God was able to put his plan into action—a plan that turned things upside down and that was to show people everywhere just how much God loves them.

Unlike Mary, we know what would happen next—how Jesus would be born not in a royal palace, nor as a prince with fine clothes, but as an ordinary baby, in an ordinary family. Only a few visitors to Bethlehem such as the shepherds, Simeon and Anna in the temple and the wise men would realize that this baby was the special Messiah that God had promised—Jesus the rescuer.

At Christmas we mainly think about the time when Jesus was born as a tiny baby, but the rest of the year we can hear stories about what happened when Jesus grew up. These stories tell us about the amazing things Jesus did and said. Only then did people begin to call him 'Jesus Christ'. The word Christ means 'anointed one' or 'the anointed king' or, in Hebrew, the language of the people of Israel, 'Messiah'—the special king that God had promised to send. Not everyone believed that Jesus was the Messiah, but that is another story!

CRAFT ACTIVITY: A SPECIAL CHRISTMAS GIFT

Include the craft activity at this point if there is time. Where time is limited, move straight into candle time.

> **You will need:**
> ★ An assortment of tiny boxes (matchboxes and so on). (Children could be asked to bring in their own.)
> ★ Wrapping paper or sticky shapes and felt-tipped pens
> ★ Small old Christmas cards
> ★ Hole punch
> ★ Thread, wool or Christmas ribbon
> ★ Scissors
> ★ Clear sticky tape
> ★ Pinking shears (optional)

Carefully wrap the box in wrapping paper, covering the bottom and the lid of the box separately so that the box can still be opened. Where a matchbox is used, the outer sleeve alone could be decorated.

As an alternative to wrapping paper, children could

decorate their box with sticky shapes or colour it using felt-tipped pens. Cut a gift-size tag out of an old Christmas card using pinking shears. Punch a hole in one edge and thread ribbon through. Write on the gift tag and attach it to the box.

CANDLE TIME

Invite the children into a circle and place the Advent candle in the centre of the circle. When everyone is seated, light the candle.

If children have made boxes in their craft activity, invite them to bring the boxes into the circle. Otherwise, pass round a basket with little decorated boxes inside, one for each child.

With only a few more days left before Christmas Day, remind the children that Christmas Day is the day when we remember Jesus' birthday. Remind them that among the other presents opened on Christmas Day, there is always one very special present. This present can't be opened, but is with us all the year round. It is the gift from God that the people waited for so long—Jesus the rescuer, God's special gift of love.

Slowly pass round a second basket, this time with little heart shapes in it (use the template opposite, or heart-shaped confetti, available from card shops). Invite each child to take a heart shape from the basket; as he or she does so, everyone should say, 'God loves… *(name)*.'

When the basket has gone all the way round (to the adults as well as the children), invite everyone to hold the heart shape in the palm of their hand while one of the children reads the prayer.

PRAYER FOR THE WEEK

Dear Jesus, thank you that you came to live on earth to show us how much God loves us. Help us, like Mary, to follow in your ways and show your love to others.

Invite the children to place their heart shape into their box, as a symbol of God's special gift of love—not just at Christmas, but all the year round.

When Jesus was born as a tiny baby in Bethlehem, the Bible tells us that angels filled the sky with happy songs announcing his birth. The Bible also tells us that when Jesus comes again, all of creation will sing and shout for joy. What a special day that will be!

SHARING LIFE THROUGH ADVENT WITH FAMILIES

INTRODUCTION

Christmas can be a season fraught with activity and busyness. We can often arrive at Christmas Day having forgotten what the real celebration is about. Here are some ideas for how the whole family can make the important countdown to Christmas more meaningful and exciting. At the heart of all celebrations there is a place for:

- Story
- Symbol
- Sharing
- Remembering and often resolution

In each of the four weeks of Advent, you will see these four themes recurring. You will be encouraged to discover the significance of colour, create your own family prayers, share stories, decorate the home, prepare special foods and maybe even have time to play a game or two.

Some families may set aside a time each day to light the candle and share the ideas, maybe during a shared meal. Other families may find it easier to set aside time just once a week. Either way, with the use of the four Bible passages, candle and suggestions for different family activities, you can do as little or as much as you choose, or as time allows.

So join in the Advent journey and follow us all the way to Bethlehem!

KEY TO ACTIVITIES

Light the candle

Thinking about the story

Themes to explore

Pray together

Things to make

Games to play

Footsteps

IDEAS FOR USING THE MATERIAL

- As a family, decide whether you are going to light the candle at the meal table, or whether you are going to set up a special focus space where the candle might be placed. This might be on a special table or shelf.
- Decide when you might share this special time together. It might be at a mealtime, at bedtime or even during the weekend.
- Use a modern version of the Bible for the readings.
- Involve different members of the family in reading the Bible passage.
- Don't be afraid to repeat the reading of the same passage over several days. Different things might come out of the passage with repeated reading.
- Encourage each member of the family to contribute to any conversation about the passage or the picture if they wish to, and really listen to each other.
- In some churches, the Christian festivals are marked by special liturgical colours. This might be picked up in the clothes worn by the minister or on altar frontals or cloths. The liturgical colour for Advent is purple. As a family, you might want to mark this special time by using a purple cloth or serviettes at the table. They might be paper cloths and serviettes, or the children might like to make special place-mats decorated in purple.
- Follow the instructions and make a Christmas garland to hang on your Christmas tree or in your house. Each week there will be ideas for adding a different symbol to your garland. The finished garland will tell the story of your journey through Advent.
- Where young children are involved, take special care with the lighting and positioning of the candle. Do not leave matches where children can reach them.

YEAR A

ADVENT 1

PILGRIMAGE TO JERUSALEM

ISAIAH 2:1–5

Light the candle and read Isaiah 2:1–5. The prophet Isaiah looks to a time when people from all different countries will journey together to listen to what God has to say. It points to a time when there will be no more fighting and no more weapons of war.

Think about the story together and talk about what the writer is saying. Talk about which is your favourite part of the story.

If you are using the material daily, you could explore different themes on different days:

- **Journeys**: Share family stories of different journeys you have been on together. Remember what you each enjoyed and what you took with you.
- **Pilgrimage**: Talk about what is different about a pilgrimage. Think about how pilgrims travel to holy places to worship and to follow in the footsteps of other pilgrims. Sometimes, being a follower of Jesus is likened to being on a pilgrimage. Talk about where the pilgrims in this week's reading were going to.
- **Listening**: Talk about how we can listen to God and discover how he wants us to live.
- **Peace**: Think about countries where there is fighting. You could look at newspapers or watch the news on the TV. Imagine what it would be like if there were no more wars or people being unkind to one another.
- **Change**: This week's reading talked about a day when weapons of war would be for ever changed into useful tools. What kinds of things would you like to change in the world today?

Pray together. If you have a newspaper, you might find some pictures of people fighting or being unkind to each other. Cut the pictures out and place them on the table near the candle. Hold hands and pray for the situations in the pictures. With little children, say a few words of prayer and allow space for children to echo it.

At the end of the prayers, blow out the Advent candle.

Make a garland for your Christmas tree, which will follow your Advent journey.

You will need:
★ Strong thread
★ Egg carton
★ Large and small red beads
★ Silver foil or multi-coloured beads
★ Scissors

You might be able to find some old bead necklaces in a charity shop. If so, cut the beads off the strings, ready to rethread for your garland. Decide how long you want the garland to be and cut a length of strong thread accordingly. Knot one end and thread the beads on, making a pattern as you go with the large and small beads. Alternatively, use a ready-made string of Christmas beads.

Isaiah tells us that a time will come when there is no more need for weapons of war. What a wonderful time that will be! Add some bells to your garland to ring out the good news:

1. Cut out the cups or egg holders from the egg carton. Trim the edges and cover with silver foil.
2. Carefully cut two slits in the top of each cup, and thread some thin ribbon through the slits.
3 Hang a thread from the ribbon inside the bell and fasten on to it a small ball of rolled-up silver foil or a bead for the bell hammer.
4. Tie two or three bells to the garland and keep any extra for hanging on the Christmas tree.

Look at how you have changed the beads and egg carton into something useful and beautiful. Use the garland to remind you of how God wants us to look forward to a time when there will be no more fighting, and weapons of war will be changed into useful tools.

Without the children's knowledge, wrap up a parcel with various layers of paper. In the centre of the parcel carefully wrap the figures of Mary and Joseph. Play pass-the-parcel with the children until the figures are revealed. Explain that through Advent you are going to take Mary and Joseph on the long journey to Bethlehem.

If you normally put up a nativity scene in the home at Christmas, why not start it early this Advent by taking Mary and Joseph on their long journey to Bethlehem through your house.

Start by placing Mary and Joseph in one of the rooms of the house (perhaps one of the children's bedrooms). Decide how long Mary and Joseph will stay in each room, so that children know in advance how long Mary and Joseph can stay. Help the children to find a special place to put Mary and Joseph in their room to keep them safe until it is time to move them on. A suitable place might be on a shelf or a bedside table. As Christmas approaches, move Mary and Joseph closer and closer to where the nativity scene will be set up, so that they arrive at the place where Mary has the baby by Christmas Eve.

YEAR A

ADVENT 2

THE PEACEFUL KINGDOM

ISAIAH 11:1–10

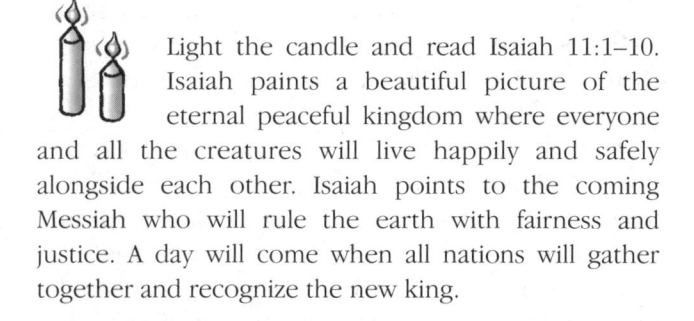

Light the candle and read Isaiah 11:1–10. Isaiah paints a beautiful picture of the eternal peaceful kingdom where everyone and all the creatures will live happily and safely alongside each other. Isaiah points to the coming Messiah who will rule the earth with fairness and justice. A day will come when all nations will gather together and recognize the new king.

Think about the story together and talk about what the writer is saying. Isaiah paints a picture with words, but what would you choose if you were painting a picture of the story?

If you are using the material daily you could explore different themes on different days.

- **Family trees**: Talk about your family tree and look at old photographs. How far can you go back in your family?
- **King David**: What do you know about King David? Jesus was to be one of his descendants. Look at 1 Samuel 16:1–13 to find out how young David was chosen to become king.
- **Judging one another**: Isaiah tells us that the Messiah will not judge people by appearance but fairly. Talk about how you judge other people. Do you find that you judge only by appearance?
- **A peaceful world**: Last week, we heard from Isaiah how one day there will be no more fighting between people in the world. This week, we hear how all of creation will one day be at peace. Talk about what this might be like. Which are your favourite creatures in God's world?
- **Children**: Look at what Isaiah says about children in this peaceful world. Talk about how you care for one another in your family.

Using a dice, give each of the numbers on the dice a different topic. For example:

1 = pray for your family
2 = pray for peace in the world
3 = thank God for something in creation
4 = pray for those who rule our country
5 = pray for anyone you know who is unwell or unhappy
6 = thank God for something special in your day

Each person takes it in turns to throw the dice and then say a short prayer about the topic that matches with the number that has been thrown. You could choose your own topics.

Doves are often used as a symbol of peace. Make some doves of peace out of salt dough, to hang on your garland and the Christmas tree.

> **You will need:**
> ★ 2 cups of plain flour
> ★ 1 cup of salt
> ★ 1 cup of water

Mix the dough together and cut out some dove shapes. Draw the shape on to card, cut it out and then use it to mark and cut out the dough, or use a biscuit cutter.

Sharing life through Advent with families

Make a small hole in the top of the dove for threading a ribbon through.

Place dove shapes on a baking sheet and bake in the oven at 150°C / 300°F / Gas Mark 2 for about an hour until the dough is hard. Paint eyes and wings on your dove and leave to dry.

Varnish with PVA glue mixed with a little water and sprinkle on some glitter before the glue dries. Thread a ribbon through the hole and hang one of the doves on your garland. Save any extra doves to hang on your Christmas tree.

Look for some old family baby photographs and give each a number between 1 and 6. Write the number on the back of each of them. There could be several pictures of the same person at different early stages.

Turn all the photographs over so that only the numbers show. Take it in turns to roll a dice and choose a photograph that matches the number. Turn the picture over and see if you can recognize who the baby is.

The winner is the one who can correctly name the most photographs. This game can be played with other relatives or friends.

Don't forget to take Mary and Joseph on the next step of their journey!

YEAR A

ADVENT 3

GOD'S SACRED HIGHWAY

ISAIAH 35:1–10

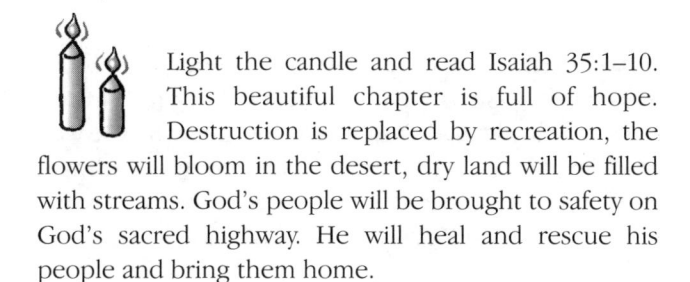

Light the candle and read Isaiah 35:1–10. This beautiful chapter is full of hope. Destruction is replaced by recreation, the flowers will bloom in the desert, dry land will be filled with streams. God's people will be brought to safety on God's sacred highway. He will heal and rescue his people and bring them home.

Think about the story together and talk about what the writer is saying. Talk about which is your favourite part of the story.

If using the material daily you could explore different themes on different days.

- **Growing things**: Talk together about what is needed for things to grow on the land. Remember and share your own stories of growing things in the garden, the allotment or the window box.
- **Deserts**: Talk together about what it might be like in the desert where nothing will grow. Think about countries where there are no rains and where crops fail year after year. How do people survive in such countries? 
- **Caring**: Talk about ways you can care for our world, to make it a better place. Talk about the different ways you can help people in poor countries, especially by buying Fair Trade products in the supermarkets.
- **Change**: Make a list together of how many things Isaiah says will be transformed in the world when the Messiah comes. Which of the changes do you most look forward to seeing happen?
- **God's sacred highway**: Talk together about what makes you feel scared and what makes you feel safe. Isaiah talks about the Messiah leading us to a safe place, but I wonder what you think that will be like?

For this week's prayers, you will need either a packet of ready-cut paper chains or some strips of different coloured paper approximately 20cm x 3cm, and some glue.

Each day, choose a different theme to pray for and invite each member of the family to write or draw their prayer on to the paper chain. Take it in turns to pray each prayer, then stick the paper chains together and watch them grow as the week goes by.

At the end of the week, use the paper chain as part of your Christmas decorations.

Themes to pray for might include:

- Thanking God for all the good things that grow in the world.
- Praying for people living in countries where the crops don't grow.
- Praying for things you would like to see changed in the world to make it a better place.
- Thanking God for each other and praying for anyone you know who is afraid, sad or lonely.
- Thanking God for Christmas.

Add some fruit to your garland to remind you of how God will change the desert into a fruitful land.

You will need:
- ★ Little fir cones
- ★ Gold poster paint and brush
- ★ Clingfilm
- ★ Nuts and raisins
- ★ Red ribbon

---

1. Paint the fir cones gold and leave them to dry.

2. Cut a small square of clingfilm and place some fruit and nuts in the centre of it. Twist the clingfilm to make a little bundle. Tie a ribbon around the top in a neat bow.
3. Using thread, attach some fir cones and the little bag of fruit and nuts along your garland.

7. Beat egg white and add icing sugar and lemon juice to make a smooth paste. Add food colouring if you wish.
8. When the biscuits are cooked and cold, decorate by spreading icing over the shape or piping patterns with a piping bag. Thread thin ribbon through the hole of the biscuit to hang it on the Christmas tree.

If you put a Christmas tree up in your home this Christmas and decorate it, you will be changing it from a bare tree to one that is beautifully decorated, maybe with twinkling lights. As you look at your tree this Christmas, remember how the Messiah wants to transform the world into a beautiful, safe and happy place.

Don't forget to take Mary and Joseph on the next step of their journey!

Make some special Christmas biscuits.

You will need:
★ 225g plain flour
★ 110g caster sugar
★ 1 tsp ground cinnamon
★ 110g margarine
★ 1 tsp ground ginger
★ 1 egg

(For icing)
★ 225g icing sugar
★ 1 tsp lemon juice
★ 1 egg white
★ Food colouring (optional)

1. Grease a baking sheet and light the oven at 180°C/350°F/Gas Mark 4.
2. Mix flour, spices and sugar together. Rub in margarine.
3. Add egg and mix to a dough.
4. Chill dough in fridge before rolling out thinly.
5. Cut shapes out of the dough using Christmas shaped biscuit cutters. Make holes in the top of the biscuits if you want to hang them on the Christmas tree.
6. Place on a baking tray and bake for 15 minutes.

YEAR A

ADVENT 4

THE NEW KING IS COMING

LUKE 1:26–38

Light the candle and read Luke 1:26–38. This is the story of the annunciation, when the angel comes to tell Mary that she is to become the mother of the long-awaited Messiah— God's special king. Mary's obedience and 'yes' to God sets into motion God's plan to show his people just how much he loves them and us.

Think about the story together and talk about what the writer is saying. Talk about which is your favourite part of the story.

If using the material daily, you could explore different themes on different days.

- **Angels**: Talk together about angels and what you think they might look like. Look up some of the stories in the Bible where angels are mentioned, such as Genesis 18:1–15; Daniel 6:1–23 and Luke 1:8–20.
- **Mary**: Talk about how you think Mary might have felt after the angel left her. What would she tell Joseph? Mary went to visit her cousin Elizabeth to tell her about the angel's news. Who might you go and talk to if you had something special to share?
- **Joseph**: Talk about how you think Joseph felt about Mary's news. Look up Matthew 1:18–25 and see how the angel also came to tell Joseph about the Messiah.
- **Expecting a baby**: Talk about what it is like waiting for a new baby to be born. What do we need to get ready? Where appropriate, share family stories about waiting for a new baby brother or sister to arrive.
- **Names**: The angel told both Mary and Joseph to call their baby Jesus. Share stories about how your names were chosen for you.

Cut out some star shapes, enough for one for each member of the family. Invite each person to write or draw a one-line prayer, thanking God for sending the gift of his son Jesus to the earth on that first Christmas. At the end of each day, the prayers could be attached to a thread to hang down as star mobiles.

Add an angel messenger to your garland. It was an angel who told Mary that she was to be the mother of God's son, the Messiah.

You will need:
★ Paper doily
★ Glue and stapler
★ Cotton wool ball
★ Scissors
★ Glitter

1. Cut a triangle out of the doily by drawing two lines from the edge of the doily to the centre.
2. Join the two edges of the remaining doily to make a cone shape for the body of the angel.
3. Fold the cut-out triangle in half and cut the top into a heart shape. Open the shape out and attach it to the angel's body for wings.
4. Glue a cotton wool ball on top to make the head. Decorate with glitter for hair.

Sharing life through Advent with families

5. Cut a small circle of card and draw the angel's face. Stick the card to the front of the cotton wool ball.
6. Attach a piece of thread to the back of the angel and hang it at the centre of the Christmas garland. Hang any extra angels on to the Christmas tree.

On a tray, place various items that tell the Christmas story.

An angel	tells Mary the good news
A donkey	carries Mary to Bethlehem
Strips of cloth	wrapped around baby Jesus
A carol sheet	the angels filled the sky with music
A woolly sheep	shepherds come to visit the baby Jesus
Some straw	laid in the manger where Jesus lies
A star	leads the wise men to the stable
Small gifts	brought by the wise men
A candle	Jesus came to be the light of the world
A heart shape	Jesus, God's special gift of love to us

Cover the items on the tray with a small white cloth and give everyone a piece of paper and a pencil. Everyone has one minute to look at the items on the tray and then the tray is covered up again. Everyone must write or draw the items they can remember seeing on the tray. Check off everyone's answers.

Now use the items on the tray to tell the Christmas story. First of all, lay the white cloth on the floor (white is the liturgical colour for Christmas). Now slowly take one item at a time off the tray, telling the story as each item is set down on the white cloth. Young children may enjoy retelling the story for themselves, using the items on the tray, over the days up to Christmas.

Don't forget to take Mary and Joseph on the last lap of their long journey to Bethlehem. It will soon be Christmas Day and time to celebrate that Jesus the Messiah is born!

SHARING LIFE THROUGH ADVENT BIBLE READING NOTES

YEAR A

ADVENT 1

PILGRIMAGE TO JERUSALEM

ISAIAH 2:1–5

KEY VERSE

People of Israel, let's live by the light of the Lord.
ISAIAH 2:5

This is a lovely reading, captured in a picture full of hope. But hope always deals with the future. The prophet wants God's people to look ahead, to a time when violence, war and conflict will be a thing of the past. This sounds like an empty hope, no more than whistling in the dark. After all, everything we know of human history and the human heart makes us sceptical about visions of a golden era to come.

However, the prophet calls his hearers, as he calls us, to set out on a journey of hope, which is really what Advent is. It's about waiting, anticipation, longing—for the coming of the Saviour, not just as he came at the first Christmas but as he will one day come again finally to bring in that era of peace and justice. It's also about movement—movement towards a goal. For Isaiah, that goal is a city that lies somewhere ahead, 'the true Zion', the community of God, the 'new Jerusalem'.

In his vision, Jerusalem (Zion) is no longer the exclusive home of one people, the Jews, but a house of peace for all nations—a community to which every single human being can belong. This won't be brought about by a religion exclusive to one people, but by a faith that shares its blessings with all.

So this reading, and the picture it offers, ask us to look beyond where we are—to be a 'people of vision'—and to look 'out' to the whole world around us. So our prayers and longings in Advent can't just be private, inward or exclusive, but should embrace the people of the whole world. Yes, that world is still war-torn, distressed, anxious... greedy, too, perhaps, and often selfish. Yet it is that world to which Jesus came, the one we expect and long for. It is that world for which we pray and in which we must try to live as his disciples. It is that world where we try to do our part in making peace and sharing its riches. It is that world which is drawn by God into the community of the 'new Jerusalem'.

TO THINK ABOUT

Are we ready for the journey towards this new community? Can we sense the longing and hope that drive feet to follow the road to the new city? What can we do to be part of the fulfilling of this vision—not just in our prayers, but changes in lifestyle, priorities and choices? Are there decisions we could make this Advent that would reflect our desire to be part of God's 'new world'?

A PRAYER

God of hope, give us this Advent a faith that looks inwards to the deepest longings of our own hearts, upwards to the heavenly city and out to the whole world. Hold before our eyes this vision of hope as we joyfully wait for the coming of the Saviour. Amen

YEAR A

ADVENT 2

THE PEACEFUL KINGDOM

ISAIAH 11:1–10

KEY VERSE

Just as water fills the sea, the land will be filled with people who know and honour the Lord.

ISAIAH 11:9

TO THINK ABOUT

The world pictured here is recognizably our world but utterly transformed in an age of peace and justice. All natural enmities are set aside. All the ancient causes of fear, like deadly snakes, are rendered harmless. Is this simply daydreaming, or can we believe that this is how God wishes to see his creation—at one with him, at one with each other? What does this say to a world of violence, terrorism and fear? How can we be part of the process of bringing this vision about?

Again we have an idyllic picture, this time of perfect peace—peace with one another, peace with the whole creation and peace with God. It is an expression of the deepest longings of the human heart, at least in our better moments. But the prophet does not suggest that this will simply 'happen'. Its coming is linked to this rather mysterious 'member of David's family' who will be filled with the Spirit of God, imbued with wisdom, understanding and power, and deep reverence for our Creator-God.

We are not told his name, but clearly he was a messianic figure, because he is a descendant of Jesse and therefore also a descendant of the great king David. Christians have from the earliest times identified him with Jesus, the Messiah sent by God to be our Saviour. It is through him that these wonderful blessings are to come to the human race.

That is why Christians can call Jesus the hope of the world. It is in him—in his love, wisdom and power—that the earth will be blessed, and blessed in such a way that one day the earth will be filled with people who know and honour the Lord, just as water fills the sea.

So these are the blessings of Advent—a world renewed, changed, transformed; a creation at peace with itself and God; and a kingdom of security and justice. Of course, some of those blessings can begin now for those who truly seek God, but they will come in fullness when people recognize this 'member of David's family', Jesus, as the world's Saviour and seek the just and gentle rule of his kingdom. Today our prayers can be for its coming, as we long and hope for the fulfilment on earth of this wonderful promise.

A PRAYER

Lord, we would like to see our world renewed into a place of peace and harmony. Renew us by your life-giving Spirit, so that we can be agents of peace, justice and love where we are, and so be part of your great purpose for the whole creation. Amen

Sharing life through Advent Bible reading notes

Reproduced with permission from *Sharing Life through Advent* published by BRF 2004 (1 84101 306 4)

YEAR A

ADVENT 3

GOD'S SACRED HIGHWAY

ISAIAH 35:1–10

KEY VERSE

A good road will be there, and it will be named 'God's Sacred Highway'.
ISAIAH 35:8

TO THINK ABOUT

Everyone would like to live in a place of gladness and joy and see the desert places changed into fertile fields. What might it ask of us to pursue this beautiful vision? How do we see 'God's sacred highway'? Is it some sort of mystical experience or religious discipline not readily accessible to most of us? Or might it be, more simply, seeking to live our lives more in line with what we know in our hearts God requires?

The vision of future blessing continues, this time built around a road, 'God's sacred highway'. It leads through a transformed desert. Where once were stones, scorching sand and dryness, there will be bubbling springs and pools. Grass, reeds and papyrus will flourish. Crocuses will blossom. Again, it is a beautiful picture of a transformed existence: 'thirsty deserts will be glad'.

Most of us don't live in actual deserts, but we may well feel that our lives are sometimes like desert places—dry, waterless and unproductive. We may long to see something blossoming there. And at any ordinary, practical level, we are all aware how seriously our planet's environment has been damaged by human exploitation, with huge tracts being turned from fertile land into deserts. So at every level this vision, like the earlier ones, is deeply relevant.

In the passage, the method by which the vision may be realized is spelt out. It is a *sacred* highway—the journey of lives lived in conformity with the will and purpose of the Creator. Those who are on the journey are called 'God's people', 'the people the Lord has rescued', the ones whose freedom has been bought by him. It's a picture of the grace and mercy of God—a picture fulfilled, of course, in the coming of Jesus, and especially in his death and resurrection, by which we are set free from the slavery of lives lived in wilful disobedience to God.

A PRAYER

God of mercy and love, set us free from the old way, the desert way, and bring us on to the sacred highway that leads to your kingdom.
Amen

Sharing life through Advent Bible reading notes

YEAR A

ADVENT 4

THE NEW KING IS COMING

LUKE 1:26–38

KEY VERSE

Mary said, 'I am the Lord's servant! Let it happen as you have said.'
LUKE 1:38

TO THINK ABOUT

It's interesting to imagine how Mary must have felt after the angel's visit—frightened, surely; but excited, perhaps, and anxious about Joseph's reaction when he learnt the news. It's also interesting to imagine the scene. What do you think we would have seen if we had been bystanders, or if the event had been filmed? Was this a private vision or a public appearance? Luke is quite clear that the angel's visit was for *her* and no one else (see vv. 27–28). Another thought: Gabriel's visit would lead to yet another journey in due course, from Nazareth to Bethlehem, about 60 miles, with Mary in the final stages of pregnancy. Advent is about journeys, as we have seen, always with the future in mind—moving onwards within and towards the final purpose of God.

This story is so familiar that the shock and impact of it may escape us. Perhaps this picture will help to focus our thoughts in a fresh way on the angelic visit to Mary, who was probably no more than fourteen or fifteen years old. One wonders if she realized, as he was speaking to her, quite how far-reaching and momentous an event this was. For her personally, of course, it was shattering enough—pregnant, but unmarried and a virgin—but it was probably a long while, perhaps not until after the resurrection of Jesus, before she was able to see that Gabriel's words were the fulfilment of an ancient promise. The baby she was to bear would be the Messiah, the 'Son of God Most High', the one the prophets had foretold and for whom, with mounting despair, the people of Israel had waited through the long centuries.

Angels are God's messengers. They don't speak on their own authority, but from God. They are also, in the biblical story, very often signs of God's presence with his people—a presence that the people of Israel had missed for many centuries under the occupation of Greeks and Romans. For Mary, and for her fiancé Joseph, Gabriel's visit and his words would change things for ever. What was required of her was an act of supreme obedience, and it says much for the simple faith of this young girl that she was able to respond with the remarkable words, 'I am the Lord's servant! Let it happen as you have said.'

A PRAYER

Grant to us, like Mary, a faith that takes you at your word and, in simple obedience, seeks to do your will. Amen

Sharing life through Advent Bible reading notes

SHARING LIFE THROUGH COLLECTIVE WORSHIP

INTRODUCTION

Advent is a time of preparation. In this sense it combines an opportunity to reflect on the past with a chance to repent and look to the future. We speak of Christmas as a time of peace and goodwill and, in the short term, Christians look forward to the celebration of the birth of Jesus and the peace he brings during Advent. Angels announcing the birth of Jesus to shepherds looking after their sheep in fields praised God and spoke of 'peace on earth'. In the longer term, Christians look beyond the celebration of Jesus' birth to the coming of a time of peace, an ideal world when the conflicts and hardships evident in today's world will have come to an end.

These outlines for collective worship look at the story of Advent from the prophecies of the Old Testament through to the fulfilment of those prophecies in the New Testament. The outlines give opportunity for the children to reflect on what happened 2000 years ago, starting with the birth of Jesus and then moving forward in the story to think about the lessons that Jesus taught and how they can speak to us today.

Each outline suggests placing a focal table at the front of the group of children, on to which can be placed different symbols linked with the week's story. Also on the table is placed a special Advent candle or Advent wreath. The candle is lit during the worship as a focus for reflection and prayer. (For instructions on how to make an Advent wreath, see page 80.

Each collective worship session ends with one or two ideas for follow-up discussions and developmental work in the classroom, but further ideas can also be drawn from the two sections, 'Sharing life through Advent with children' and 'Sharing life through Advent with families', which can be found on pages 14 and 22 of this book respectively.

✶

ADVENT 1: PILGRIMAGE TO JERUSALEM

ISAIAH 2:1–5

INTRODUCTION: WORKING FOR PEACE

This first assembly invites the children to consider ways in which people work to bring about peace in a troubled world and how everyone can be a peacemaker in their own situations.

FOCUS

The focus is a table covered with a purple cloth. In the centre of the table, place an Advent wreath.

Welcome the children and ask them if they know what time of year it is. Invite them to share what they think the candles represent. Explain how Advent means 'coming' and is the time in the Christian calendar when we get ready to celebrate the birthday of Jesus. There are four weeks in Advent, hence the four candles.

Purple is the colour the church uses to represent a time of preparation. Ask the children if they have seen other signs, such as special lights, a special tree, special music and so on, that show it is time to get ready to celebrate Christmas.

Christmas is the time when we remember how God sent his promised son, Jesus, into the world. Jesus came into the world as a tiny baby. The people of the time were expecting God to send a great king, but Jesus wasn't born in a big palace. His parents were just ordinary people. This was all part of God's plan. When Jesus grew up, he would continue to surprise people with the things that he did and said. He would show people how God wants everyone to live at peace with one another. Today we can still learn from Jesus' teaching.

Many people, who were known as prophets, spoke about Jesus' coming. One such prophet was a man called Isaiah. Isaiah spoke about a time he believed would come when all wars would end and the whole world would live in peace. He based his picture around the holy city of Jerusalem, which was the capital city of the people of Israel. Jerusalem means 'city of peace'. Today, people still long for that city to know the peace of which Isaiah spoke.

Introducing the Bible story

Read the following verses from Isaiah:

> *God will settle arguments between nations. They will beat their swords and their spears into rakes and shovels; they will never make war or attack one another. People of Israel, let's live by the light of the Lord.*
> ISAIAH 2.4–5

God will put an end to wars and arguments. People will use their swords and spears to make tools which will help feed and care for the world. People will never need to fight again.

Reflect on events in the year that have not been peaceful. Talk about conflicts and troubles that pupils have been aware of in the news. Talk also about conflicts and arguments within the school, the classroom, or the playground—God is also concerned about those times when we don't look out for one another.

REFLECTION

Jesus is often called the light of the world. This image reminds us that he shows people a better way to live. Invite a child to light the first candle on the Advent wreath. Pause and invite the children to look at the light and to think about the times when they haven't been kind to one another.

PRAYER

Father, you have given us skills and talents. Teach us to use them to live in peace in your world, so that it can be a better place for everyone.

SONGS

Make me a channel of your peace
Peace is flowing like a river

SUPPLEMENTARY STORY

Christian Aid reported that as many as seven million guns are thought to have been buried all over Mozambique following the country's civil war, which ended in 1992. Many soldiers hid their guns in order either to use them again or sell them. Gradually these guns are being found. It is important to destroy them so that people cannot use them to rob others in this country where many are very poor.

Since 1994, more than 100,000 weapons have been destroyed. When people hand them in, they get tools in return, such as sewing machines or ploughs, to help them earn an honest living. The weapons are cut up and given to artists who make sculptures, chairs and other useful things from them.

✳

ADVENT 2: THE PEACEFUL KINGDOM

ISAIAH 11:1–10

INTRODUCTION

This assembly explores the idea that we should not judge others by appearance, and that the Christian hope is that all peoples can live in harmony.

FOCUS

The focus is a table covered with a purple cloth, with the Advent wreath placed in the centre. On a separate table, place animal masks illustrating the different animals mentioned in the Bible reading from Isaiah, plus items that look very different on the inside from the outside, such as a shell with a rough outside and smooth, shiny, beautiful inside; a conker that is prickly on the outside and smooth and shiny when removed from its covering; or an apple that is red and shiny on the outside and white and juicy on the inside.

Welcome the children and begin by showing them the things that look very different on the inside and outside. Talk about how the outside of the items does not prepare you for what you find inside. People can be like this too. What they look like on the outside is only a small part of who they are on the inside. What is on the inside is far more important.

The prophet Isaiah painted a beautiful word-picture describing what the future might look like in a world where the whole of creation lives together at peace.

Introducing the Bible story

Read Isaiah 11:1–10. As the Bible passage is read, invite the children to close their eyes and imagine what Isaiah's peaceful world might look like.

REFLECTION

Invite a child to light the first and second candles on the Advent wreath.

PRAYER

Father, you have made us each unique and special. Teach us to live in harmony with our brothers and sisters, so that the world can be a better place for everyone.

SONGS

Cross over the road
I am special

SUPPLEMENTARY STORY

You might retell this story by Anthony de Mello. A young black boy watches a balloon seller. As people buy balloons, they are released to soar high into the sky. The boy asks whether a black balloon will soar as high as the others. The balloon seller, understanding the real question, releases a black one and tells the boy, 'It isn't the colour, son, it's what's inside the balloon that makes it rise into the air.'

✸

ADVENT 3: GOD'S SACRED HIGHWAY

ISAIAH 35:1–10

INTRODUCTION: A TRANSFORMED WORLD

This assembly looks at ways in which people are working to improve the environment and living conditions in all sorts of places, and ways in which we can all play a part in looking after the world in which we live. The prophet Isaiah sees this transformation as 'God's sacred highway', a good road where people may walk safely and in peace.

FOCUS

The focus is a table covered with a purple cloth, with a candle or the Advent wreath in the centre. On the floor in front of the table, place some attractive plants.

Welcome the children and begin by talking about the plants and what they need to enable them to grow. Ask the children to imagine living in a country where no plants, trees, grass or flowers grow. Talk about the kinds of places where plants do not grow successfully and what is lacking in those places. Go on to consider how people's crops fail in areas where there is not enough water and fertile soil and where the people suffer from hunger and starvation.

Introducing the Bible story

The prophet Isaiah spoke of a time when this kind of suffering would be at an end because even the deserts would be fertile and full of beauty. Read Isaiah 35:1–10.

The desert will be a happy and beautiful place and flowers will bloom there. The desert will sing and shout for joy and streams of water will flow through the desert.

REFLECTION

Invite two children to the front of the group and offer them two glasses of water, one containing clean water and the other 'dirty' water made by mixing gravy browning into the water. Ask the children which glass they would rather drink from.

Place the two glasses of water on the focus table. Invite the two children to light the three candles on the Advent wreath.

Invite all the children to think about people who are forced to live with sickness, hunger and hardship because there is not enough clean water.

PRAYER

Father, you have made the world very beautiful. Teach us to love our world and take care of it, so that it can be a better place for everyone.

SONGS

Thank you for every new good morning
Shalom
Peace is flowing like a river

SUPPLEMENTARY STORY

Explore ways in which people today are striving to bring clean water to areas which have none and so make it easier and safer for people to live there.

Tell the story of Alemitu. Alemitu is a little girl who longs to go to school in the same way that her brothers do, but she is unable to do so because where she lives it is the job of women and girls to collect all the water needed by the household. It takes her and her mother one and a half hours to walk to the water, and another one and a half hours to walk back. They both have to do this twice a day. With six hours taken up in this way, there is no opportunity for Alemitu to go to school.

One day, people arrive to dig a well for the village and everyone is very excited. The greatest excitement for Alemitu is that, at last, she no longer needs to spend so much time collecting water, so she is able to go to school and have the chance to improve her life further.

FROM *VALUES AND VISIONS*, MANCHESTER DEVELOPMENT EDUCATION PROJECT, HODDER AND STOUGHTON, 1996

ADVENT 4: THE NEW KING IS COMING

LUKE 1:26–38

INTRODUCTION

This assembly reflects on how Mary's life was changed when she was chosen to be the mother of Jesus, and how God can change anyone's life.

FOCUS

The focus is a table covered with a purple cloth, with the Advent wreath in the centre. Around the wreath, place figures of Mary and the angel Gabriel taken from a nativity set.

Welcome the children and remind them that we shall soon be celebrating Christmas—the birthday of Jesus. In this act of worship, however, the focus is going to be on Mary, Jesus' mother. Talk about how Mary was an ordinary young woman, living an ordinary life in first-century Palestine. Then, one day, something happened to Mary that changed her whole life. God told her he wanted her to have a very special baby. This baby was God's own son.

Introducing the Bible story

Read Luke 1:26–38.

When the angel visited Mary, she was confused by his words and wondered what it was all about. But the angel said, 'Don't be afraid, Mary. God wants you to have a very special baby. His name will be Jesus. He will be great. He will be known as the Son of God.' Mary said to the angel, 'How can all this happen to me?' The angel replied, 'With his power God can make anything happen.' Mary said, 'I will do whatever God wants.' Then the angel left her.

Invite the children to talk about the story. Think together about ways in which Mary's life would have changed, in terms of having a baby and becoming the mother of the son of God. How would Mary have felt? Might she have been excited, frightened, nervous? Talk about how these are the kinds of feelings everyone has when starting something new or unexpected.

God changed Mary's life. Her story is very famous. Artists and sculptors have painted her and made statues of her. Many churches, schools and roads are named after her. Perhaps your school is named after her!

REFLECTION

Reflect upon the way in which things changed because Jesus came into the world. Jesus showed people how God wanted them to live, and many people listened. In what ways is life as it is today because of what Jesus taught? At this time of year, in celebration of his birth, many Christians give a great deal of thought to what Jesus taught and try especially hard to live as God wants.

Remember together the themes explored in the previous three weeks. As each theme of Advent is remembered, invite a child to light a candle on the Advent wreath.

Advent 1: We need to work for peace in the world.
Advent 2: We need to get on with people who are different from us.
Advent 3: We need to help to make the world a better place and remember those in the world who are forced to live with sickness, hunger and hardship.
Advent 4: We need to make a difference in the world. When Mary said 'yes' to God, her willingness to do what God wanted made a huge difference.

Reflect on what might happen if we tried our hardest to live as God wanted. What could we do to bring about peace, to get on better with people, to help make the world a better place and to make a difference?

PRAYER

When we think of Mary, we remember that she was just an ordinary person. Help us to remember that each one of us is a child of God. We are all meant to shine. Help us to do what is good and right, to show your love in the world.

SONGS

Mary had a baby
Christmas-related carols

SUPPLEMENTARY STORY

There are many stories of people whose lives have been changed by an encounter with God. Biblical examples include Zacchaeus in Luke 19:1–10 and the apostle Paul in Acts 9:1–19.

Examples of people in history who felt called to a particular kind of work in the service of God might include Dr Barnardo and William Booth. *Stories of Everyday Saints* by Veronica Heley (published by BRF) has many stories that you might like to use to illustrate how people can make a difference by the way they live their lives. There may also be people in your own locality who could be invited to speak about their experiences of being called by God.

★ ★ ★ YEAR B ★ ★ ★

PROMISES

SHARING LIFE THROUGH WORSHIP

INTRODUCTION

Advent is a time of waiting and anticipation. It's a time when we look back to all that God has done through his people over the centuries. It's the time when we celebrate again the birth of the promised Messiah and, in the light of his love, examine afresh our own lives and readiness to meet him when he comes again.

The focus for this year's Advent readings points to God's promises, past, present and future. The first of the three readings from Isaiah follows the path of the people of Israel into exile in Babylon and to their eventual return to Jerusalem. Through the passages we see God's constant loving and faithful response to his people. We see his father-heart, which moulds our lives like clay in the potter's hands, and the shepherd who gathers and tends his flock, bringing even the weakest safely home.

The third Sunday of Advent heralds good news for all people—first of all, as God promises to restore his chosen people to Jerusalem; and then, later, in the message of John the Baptist who echoes the prophet Isaiah's words in announcing the coming of the Messiah. The fourth Sunday of Advent brings more good news as God's promise moves a step closer to fulfilment with the visit of the angel to Mary. But always the story points to the path ahead and the glorious promise that one day Christ will return. In the words of the prophet Isaiah, 'The Lord will bring about justice and praise in every nation on earth, like flowers blooming in a garden' (Isaiah 61:11).

AN ADVENT SIGNPOST POINTS THE WAY

The visual focus for this Advent is a signpost. This could be a simple construction placed in a central position (ideally where the nativity scene will be placed in Advent 4). If the church has a wooden cross for Good Friday, this might be used. Advent candles could also be lit at this focal point. If it is not possible to make a simple construction, a large picture or OHP acetate might be used instead.

We often take signposts for granted. Signposts are just there: we rely on them to show us the right path to follow and we trust them to be true. Imagine, as in wartime Britain, that all signposts were removed. How would we find the way?

The Advent signpost has two arms, one pointing to the past and the other to the future. The post itself points to the ground where you are standing and marks the present. This is the starting point for this Advent. We can pause to look at the past, consider where we are in the present and look forward to the promises of what is to come. Our response to the past and the present may well affect our hopes and our purposes for the future. The shape of the signpost deliberately mirrors the shape of the cross, the point to which we must all come on the journey. (See page 45 for a picture of the signpost.)

FOCAL AREAS FOR REFLECTION AND RESPONSE

Each week of Advent there will be the opportunity for further private reflection and response to the week's readings in the four focus areas described below. These could be used corporately as part of a reflective prayer time during the service, individually after the service, or as a focus for home group or midweek services.

Each week a new focus area can be set up, adding to those of previous weeks. Depending on the layout and facilities of the church, each focus area could be set up in different spaces around the church, making use of natural spaces such as the lady chapel, an alcove or the font. Areas may be visited on more than one week and by the fourth week in Advent each area might be visited in the form of a journey, individually or corporately visiting each area in procession. The journey mirrors that travelled by Mary and Joseph on their way to Bethlehem—a journey ending at the stable, at the feet of the Christ-child.

SUGGESTIONS FOR THE FOUR FOCAL AREAS

Advent 1: Like clay in the potter's hand

> *You, Lord, are our Father. We are nothing but clay, but you are the potter who moulded us.*
> ISAIAH 64:8

The focus might include:

- Cloth for table
- Variety of clay pots and lamps or pictures
- Small balls of clay in a bowl (covered with clingfilm to keep them pliable)
- Modelling tools
- Bucket of water, soap and towel
- The Bible verse photocopied on to small cards, enough for every member of the congregation

Photocopy these words of instruction and invitation on to a card and lay it on the table.

> Take time to look at the different pots. What size or shape of pot represents how you feel today?
>
> Take a ball of clay and imagine yourself in God's hands. Close your eyes and mould the clay as you feel God is leading you.
>
> Take your pot home and place it where you can readily see it throughout Advent. You might want to incorporate a nightlight or candle into your pot to remind you that Jesus came to be the light of the world. With his help we too are called to shine as lights in the world.

Advent 2: Get ready to be rescued!

> *The Lord cares for his nation, just as shepherds care for their flocks. He carries the lambs in his arms, while gently leading the mother sheep.*
> ISAIAH 40:11

The focus might include:

- Cloth for table
- Chunky candle
- Metal chain to wrap around candle
- Strips of gummed paper chains
- Pens
- The Bible verse photocopied on to small cards, enough for every member of the congregation

Photocopy these words of instruction and invitation on to a card and lay it on the table.

> Take time to think about those things in your life that separate you from God, and those things that bind others. Take a paper chain strip and join it together or link to existing chain links.
>
> God knows the thoughts of our hearts and forgives those who sincerely confess.
>
> Take a card with the words from Isaiah to remind you that God cares for you, just as a shepherd cares for his sheep.

If this activity is used as part of an act of worship, it could be used as the confession. The joined links could be held by those present and, as absolution is given, the chains could be pulled apart and broken, symbolic of forgiveness of sins and freedom from captivity.

Advent 3: Spread the good news

> *The Lord has sent me to comfort those who mourn... He sent me to give them flowers in place of their sorrow, olive oil in place of tears, and joyous praise in place of broken hearts.*
> ISAIAH 61:2B–3

The focus might include:

- Rug for the floor, and cushions
- Green foliage arrangement in oasis
- Globe or map of the world
- Magazine or newspaper pictures of people in pain and sadness
- Flowers (real or artificial) or flower picture and crayons
- The Bible verse photocopied on to small cards, enough for every member of the congregation

Photocopy these words of instruction and invitation on to a card and lay it on the table.

> Think about a situation in the world or at home where you know there is sorrow, tears and broken hearts. Pray for that particular situation, holding it in God's love.
>
> Take a flower and place it in the green arrangement to represent the transforming power of God's promises as spoken in Isaiah 61:2b–3.
>
> Together we pray for a broken world, looking forward to the time when Christ will come again and make all things new.

Alternatively, on the floor next to the map of the world, have a large simple flower outline with many petals. As you pray for a particular situation, colour in a petal and write the name of the place or the concern in the petal. (You may wish to use the template opposite for this.)

Advent 4: Some very special news

> *Mary said, 'I am the Lord's servant! Let it happen as you have said.'*
> LUKE 1:38

The focus might include:

- Blue cloth for table
- Picture of the annunciation
- Fragranced candle
- Coloured glass nuggets scattered on table
- Glass or wooden bowl
- The Bible verse photocopied on to small cards, enough for every member of the congregation

Photocopy these words of instruction and invitation on to a card and lay it on the table.

> Mary said 'yes' to God and God was able to fulfil his purpose through her.
>
> Choose a glass nugget from the table and hold it in the palm of your hand.
>
> With open hands and heart, think about whether God is asking you to say 'yes' to him to fulfil his purpose through you today.

> As you say your own 'yes' to God, place the nugget in the bowl.
>
> Reflect on other nuggets already in the bowl— other individuals' responses to God.
>
> Together we can work to bring God's peace on earth today.

CHRISTMAS DAY

On Christmas Day, at the foot of the signpost we find the nativity, for the nativity is past, present and future. We retell the story of long ago, witnessing the fulfilment of God's promise to send his son to live in the world. We visit the Christ-child today, celebrating his birth and making our own offerings, confident that through his Spirit Christ is still with us. And we look to the future, for the future has been placed in our hands as we wait expectantly for the fulfilment of the promise that one day Christ will come again.

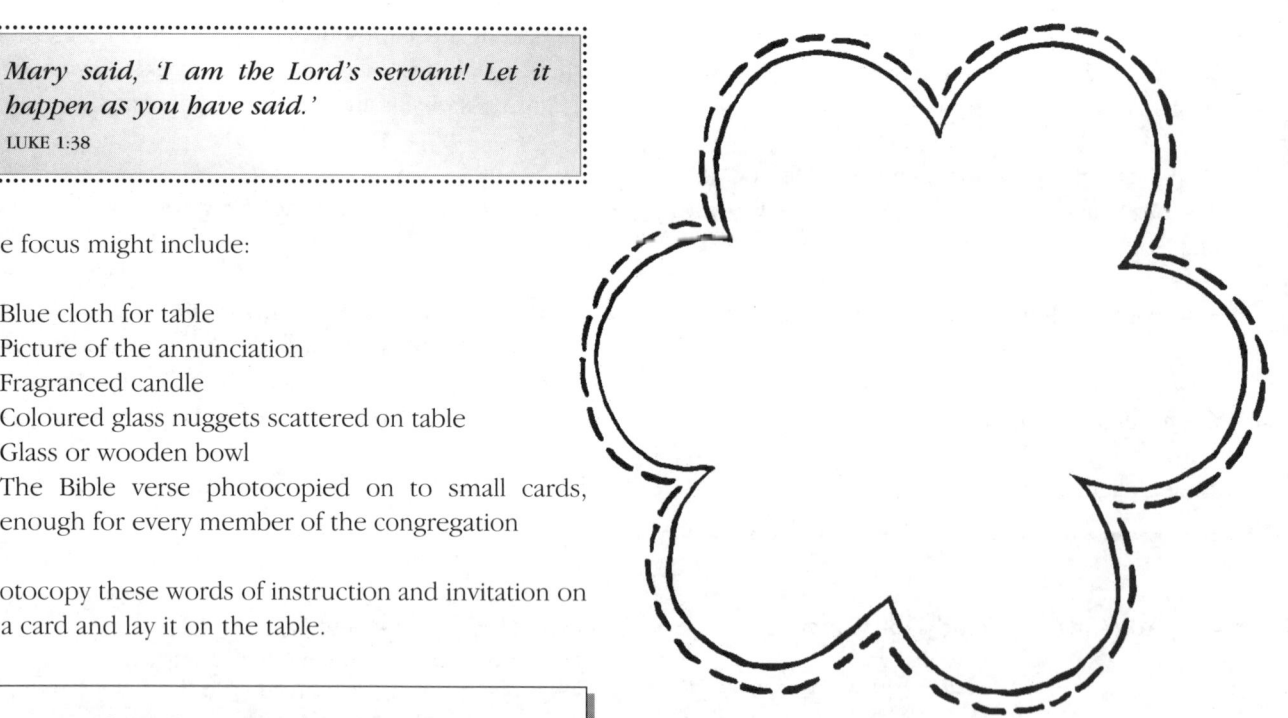

Reproduced with permission from *Sharing Life through Advent* published by BRF 2004 (1 84101 306 4)

SHARING LIFE THROUGH ADVENT WITH CHILDREN

INTRODUCTION

Advent is a time of getting ready to celebrate the mystery of Christmas, when God sent his son Jesus to live on earth among us. It is a time that links the past, the present and the future.

Imagine going for a walk and coming to a signpost pointing in two directions. On the signpost are written three words:

- Past (pointing to the path you've just come down)
- Future (pointing to the path ahead)
- Present (pointing straight down to the point at which you are standing)

Advent is a time when we look back and think about God's story of love. We remember how God sent his son Jesus to live on earth to teach us how to love and care for one another. It's the time when we look at our own lives and wonder if we are doing all that we can to bring about God's kingdom here on earth today. And finally, Advent is the time when we look forward to the future, to all that God promises is still to come.

During this Advent, there will be the opportunity to look at the bigger picture of God's love for his people, through the prophecies of Isaiah. Beginning at creation, we will journey with the people of God into exile. We'll see God's forgiveness of them, and the promise of their rescue and return home to Jerusalem.

It is Isaiah who first points the people to the coming of the promised Messiah. John the Baptist then takes up the cry as he brings the good news to the people of his day. Finally, we remember how the angel Gabriel brought the good news to Mary. Now we too can join in the story as once again, like so many before us, we celebrate the fulfilment of all that God promised on Christmas Day.

The great and glorious city of Jerusalem was the holy city where the people of Israel had settled after their many years of wandering in the desert. A line of kings ruled over them. Some, such as King David, kept God's promises but many of the kings turned from God and the people turned with them.

Over the years, the people turned more and more from God and the laws of Moses. They began to worship other gods and ignored God's teachings. So the time came when a king from another land came to Jerusalem with his army. He wanted the holy city for himself, so he and his army took it from the people of Israel. The armies burned the temple, the house of God, and they tore down the city walls. The people of Israel were taken from their beautiful holy city to a strange land—the land of Babylon. They could not go home. They were in exile, just like refugees.

In the years that followed, God chose many people to be his special messengers, or prophets. Isaiah was a prophet and he reminded the people about God's laws and about God's promise that one day he would send a special king to rescue them.

✶

ADVENT 1: LIKE CLAY IN THE POTTER'S HAND

ISAIAH 64:1–9

WONDERING

Reflect with the children about the word 'Advent' and what it means. You may wish to refer to the Introduction to help you with your ideas. Advent is a time when we can look at the big picture of God's love for us. Today we start by looking back to the very beginning of the story, to remember how God made us. This time we hear the story from Isaiah, who was a prophet—one of God's specially chosen messengers. Isaiah talks about God being like a potter (v. 8) and people being like the clay in the potter's hand.

Give each of the children a small piece of clay and invite them to mould it as you are talking. Ask the children to mould their shape into a little person. While they are modelling, ask them these questions.

- How does the clay feel?
- How easy is it to get the shape you want?
- Are you happy with your person shape?
- How do you feel when the shape goes wrong?

While the children are still modelling, read these words from Genesis 2:7.

> *The Lord God took a handful of soil and made a man. God breathed life into the man, and the man started breathing.*

Reflect with the children on their clay shapes. Imagine what it would be like to be able to breathe life into your clay shape.

'I wonder how God felt when he breathed life into that first person?

'When God made people, he could have made them like robots that he could control, but that wasn't what God did. Instead he gave people the freedom to make their own choices. He tried to show people how to live with one another and he wanted them to stay close to him, but instead they chose to go their own way. People chose not to listen to God, although when things got really bad they would go back to God and ask for his help again. Today's reading is about one of those times.'

Read Isaiah 64:5.

> *You help all who gladly obey and do what you want, but sin makes you angry. Only by your help can we ever be saved.*

Ask the children to think about times when their parents or those who care for them tell them to do something and they ignore it and do things their own way. What happens? (Words such as 'told off', 'punished', 'grounded' and so on may emerge.)

Ask the children if they think their parents or carers still love them when they are disobedient. Of course they do—and they continue to love them. It is the same with God. Like the very best kind of parent, he forgives us when we get things wrong. That is why the prophet Isaiah reminds the people that God is their father and he will forgive them.

Isaiah also uses another image to help the people understand how God cares for them. He tells them that God is like a potter and the people are like the clay in the potter's hands. Read Isaiah 64:8.

> *You, Lord, are our Father. We are nothing but clay, but you are the potter who moulded us.*

'When the potter is shaping the pot, he doesn't throw the clay away if it goes wrong. Instead he screws it back into a ball and starts again.'

At this point invite the children to roll their clay shape back into a ball.

'In the same way, God doesn't throw us away as being useless when we get things wrong. He simply reshapes us until we are the beautiful and useful people he wants us to be. But he does want us to say sorry when we get things wrong.'

PICTURING THE BIBLE

Read Isaiah 64:1–9 and talk about what the writer is saying. You might like to use some of these reflection pointers to help with the discussion.

- I wonder what the potter is shaping on the wheel?
- I wonder what the potter is thinking as he shapes the pot?
- I wonder what else you would include if you were painting a picture of the story?
- I wonder if you have ever seen a potter at work?
- I wonder if you have ever had a chance to try to spin a pot on a potter's wheel?

SETTING THE SCENE

At the time when Isaiah was writing, everybody needed pots, so the potter was kept very busy in the towns and villages. In Old Testament times the potter spun the wheel with his feet, leaving both hands free to shape the pot. If the pot spoilt in his hands, the potter started again with the same clay, reshaping it until it was the shape he wanted it to be. The pot was left to dry and then decorated before it was put into a very hot oven called a kiln, where it was baked hard. The potter made pots in all shapes and sizes for cooking, carrying water and as lamps.

God really wanted the people to know how much he loved them. He promised that one day he would send someone special into the world to show them how to live. Advent is the time when we remember how God kept his promise and sent his son Jesus into the world as a baby.

Jesus was often called the 'light of the world', the one who would help to show the way between what is right and what is wrong. There would have been no electricity in those early days, so the potter would have made lamps out of clay for people to use in their houses. The clay lamps would have been filled with oil to give light.

Invite the children to take their ball of clay and reshape it into a clay lamp, remembering to keep reshaping it until it is just how they want it.

CRAFT ACTIVITY: CLAY LAMPS

You will need:
★ Self-hardening clay
★ Rolling pins
★ Modelling tool or cocktail stick
★ Circle template, 8cm diameter
★ Tealight candles

1. Give each child a piece of the clay. Mould it until it is soft, then roll out until about 3mm thick.
2. Cut a circle of clay.
3. Gently lift the edges of the circle, folding them all the way round to form a bowl.
4. Pull the sides to meet, to create the lamp shape. Press the front edges together (see diagram below).
5. Decorate with the modelling tool or cocktail stick.
6. Leave a hole big enough to place the tealight candle in. Leave clay to harden and add tealight candle.

You may like to make four extra clay lamps for use in the four weeks of Advent during candle time.

NB: Remind the children never to light the candle unless accompanied by an adult.

CANDLE TIME

Gather the children into the circle. Place a lamp made out of clay on the floor in the centre of the circle. Place a tealight in the lamp. Invite the children to place their clay lamps on the floor in front of where they are sitting. Light the candle in the first clay lamp.

Jesus tells us to shine as lights in the world, choosing those things that are right over those that are wrong. Invite an adult to light each of the children's tealights in turn, naming the child and saying the following words: '(Name)… shine as a light in the world.'

Include any adults in the naming.

If the group is large, divide the children into smaller circles with an adult in each circle. Pause.

PRAYER FOR THE WEEK

Dear Lord Jesus, help us to shine as lights in the world for you, in our homes, in school, in the playground and wherever we are. Amen

ADVENT 2: GET READY TO BE RESCUED!

ISAIAH 40:1–11

SETTING THE SCENE

The story of the exile reminds us of how the people of Israel were taken from their homes in Jerusalem to a strange land called Babylon. They longed to go home. The prophet Isaiah listened to God and told the people what God had to say to them. Sometimes the people listened and sometimes they laughed and ignored the message. One day Isaiah came with a special message. Would the people listen this time?

Play the game 'Sheep in the mud'. Choose one or two children to be sheep dogs depending on the size of the group. Tell the rest of the children that they are sheep. On the word 'go', the sheep scatter and the dogs chase them to try to round them up. When the dog tags a sheep, the sheep must stand still with their legs apart, crying 'baa' loudly. Tagged sheep may only be rescued by a free sheep crawling through their legs. The game ends when all the sheep are static and bleating!

WONDERING

After the game, talk about what it felt like being tagged and having to stay in one place, waiting to be set free. Talk together about other experiences of being rescued—for example, getting stuck, locked in, trapped or lost. What did it feel like to be stuck? What did it feel like to be rescued?

Tell the children the story of how the people of Israel had been taken as prisoners from Jerusalem to the land of Babylon. You may wish to refer to the introduction on page 45 for ideas. Seventy years passed and the people of Israel longed to go home. Then they heard these words.

> 'Encourage my people! Give them comfort. Speak kindly to Jerusalem and announce: Your slavery is past...' Look! The powerful Lord God is coming to rule with his mighty arm... The Lord cares for his nation, just as shepherds care for their flocks. He carries the lambs in his arms, while gently leading the mother sheep.
> ISAIAH 40:1–2, 10–11

PICTURING THE BIBLE

The long wait to go home was over!

Read Isaiah 40:1–11 and talk about what the writer is saying. You might like to use some of the reflection pointers to help with the discussion.

- I wonder what the people felt when they heard they were going home?
- I wonder if they were afraid to go back to Jerusalem?
- I wonder how they felt when they got there?
- I wonder how they would feel about rebuilding their city?
- I wonder if they would be faithful to God when they got back to Jerusalem?

Have available some pictures of refugees:

- People who are afraid to go home
- People who have left their homes because of the fighting and who are now afraid to return
- Children whose parents have been killed in the fighting

Talk about the pictures and how, even today, people have to leave their homes when they don't want to. Maybe they are afraid to stay because of the threat of being hurt or even killed. These things happen in our world today when we don't care for one another as God wants us to. Many of today's refugees long to go home, but are too afraid.

CRAFT ACTIVITIES

Chains

Make two sets of chains, one representing the things that the people had done wrong, that led to their being taken as slaves to Babylon; the second a chain of sheep representing the people of Israel being rescued by God.

Chains of captivity (older children)

> You will need:
> ★ Dark coloured paper chain strips
> ★ Pens

On the back of each paper chain strip, write one thing that is an unkind or hurtful thing to do to others—for example, stealing, telling lies, fighting, calling people names and so on. When all the strips have words on the back, stick the two ends of each strip together, threading one chain to the next until you have a long chain of captivity.

Chains of freedom (younger children)

You will need:
* Templates of sheep (various sizes)
* White card
* Cotton wool
* Length of ribbon or tape
* Scissors
* Glue sticks
* Double-sided tape

Draw round the sheep templates and cut out the sheep. Stick on some cotton wool. Draw the sheep's faces. Attach the sheep to the ribbon or tape with double-sided tape to make a chain.

CANDLE TIME

Invite the children back into the circle. In the centre of the circle have a large fat candle and a clay lamp from Advent 1. Have a fresh tealight candle in the lamp. Use the following words and actions.

'God made us all and gave us the freedom to make our own choices.'

Light the tealight candle.

'But the people of Israel chose to ignore God.'

Blow out the candle in the lamp. Pause. Invite the children to name some of the things the people of Israel did to ignore God.

'God never gives up on the people of Israel. He still loved them.'

Light the fat candle.

'Today we still choose to ignore God.'

Lay the chains of captivity around the bottom of the candle. Pause.

'Bad things happen in our world today when we don't care for one another as God wants us to. Remember the places in the world today where there is fighting and wars. Think about people who are unhappy. Think about times when we do things wrong and hurt others.'

'When we say we are sorry to someone for hurting them, it often makes us feel better. We no longer feel sad. When we say sorry to God, we can also feel better and we can be sure that God forgives us.'

Sorry prayer

Father God, we are sorry when we get things wrong and hurt you and other people. Help us to make good choices about the way we treat one another. Amen

Take the chains from around the candle so that everyone can hold them. Together, break them apart. Replace the chains of captivity with the chain of sheep—a chain of freedom. Say 'thank you' to God that he forgives us, cares for us, and watches over us, just like the shepherd cares for his sheep.

✳

ADVENT 3: SPREAD THE GOOD NEWS

ISAIAH 61:1–4, 8–11; JOHN 1:6–8, 19–28

INTRODUCTION

Put balloons at the door as the children arrive and have some lively music playing. Give a sense of celebration with party whistles and party poppers. Around the room, have news articles or posters advertising good news.

As the children arrive, invite them to design their own 'good news' poster. Invite them to share a piece of good news about the past week or something that they are looking forward to. Give the children brightly coloured A4 paper to work on.

As the children complete the posters, invite them to sit in a circle. When everyone is settled, share a drink and a special biscuit or cake. (Check the children's health records for allergies or diabetes.) Talk together about the children's good news stories and expand with other examples of good news.

SETTING THE SCENE

Remind the children of the story about how God made the first people, and how the people turned away from the things God taught them. Place the clay lamp from week 1 on the floor and light the candle. The people had to say 'sorry'. Pause.

Recap the story of how the people of God had been taken as prisoners to a strange land. But God had promised that he was going to gather them together and take them home again. Place a second clay lamp on the floor and light the candle. The people said 'sorry' and God forgave them. Pause.

Now at last the people of God had some good news—they were going home to rebuild their city of Jerusalem.

Many years later, a man called John came with some more good news. He echoed the words of the prophet Isaiah when he said, 'Get the road ready for the Lord!' (John 1:23). Here was John, telling the people that at last God's own son was coming very soon. Like the prophets before him, John told the people to say 'sorry' to God for the things they had done wrong and, as a special sign of God's forgiveness, John baptized the people in the river Jordan. The people began to think that John was God's promised new king, but John assured the people that he wasn't. In fact, he said of himself, 'Even though I came first, I am not good enough to untie his sandals' (John 1:27).

PICTURING THE BIBLE

Read John 1:6–8 and 19–28 and talk about the story. You might like to use some of the reflection pointers to help with the discussion.

- I wonder what the people thought of John?
- I wonder if they knew who he was?
- I wonder how the people felt when they went into the river to be baptized?
- I wonder if you've been baptized?
- I wonder how different your baptism was from what is described in the story?

Place a clay lamp in the centre of the circle and light the candle. Say the following words:

'John told the good news that Jesus was coming. *(Pause.)* This Advent we remember how God kept his promises to the people as we celebrate Jesus' birthday. The prophet Isaiah said, "The Lord will bring about justice and praise in every nation on earth, like flowers blooming in a garden."' (Isaiah 61:11)

CRAFT ACTIVITY: GOOD NEWS SEED HEADS

While John was in the desert, he wore clothes made of camel hair, which must have been very uncomfortable. He ate locusts and wild honey and probably looked pretty wild himself. To remind you of the good news Isaiah and John brought to the people, you could make a good news seed head.

You will need:
* Plastic or foam disposable drinking cup
* Potting compost
* Spoon
* Seeds (cress or other quick-growing herb seeds)
* Water
* Sticky paper shapes
* Thin card
* Pipe cleaner

1. Carefully push the pipe cleaner through the cup, about half way down, to make John's arms. Fold in the ends to make two hands.
2. Using sticky paper, add the face of John the Baptist.
3. Cut out two feet shapes from card to stick to the bottom of the cup for John's feet.
4. Carefully fill the cups with compost, being careful not to dislodge the arms. Sprinkle some cress seeds on top and gently push them into the compost. Add a little water.

As the seeds grow, they will look like John's wild hair.

Remind the children that they will need to water and care for their seeds in order for them to grow. In the same way, we have to give time to God if we want to find out more about him and for our love for him to grow.

PRAYER FOR THE WEEK

Dear Jesus, help us in the business of getting ready for Christmas to remember that it is your birthday. Help us to share the good news with our friends and families of how you came to earth to show us how to care for one another. Amen

ADVENT 4: SOME VERY SPECIAL NEWS

LUKE 1:26–38 AND 39–45

SETTING THE SCENE

After years of waiting, God prepared to fulfil his promise to the people of Israel by sending the promised king, his own son Jesus, to live on earth.

You will need:
* Five equilateral triangles in card or felt, each side measuring 14 cms. (The colours need to be white, blue, red, purple and green.)
* One pentagon shape to fit in the centre of the triangles, made of gold felt or card.
* Woolly sheep (see template on page 49)
* Model or picture of flat-roofed house
* Small nativity figures of Mary, Joseph and an angel
* Small item made of wood
* Small crown or crown shape
* Tealight candle
* Basket or flat box to put the pieces in

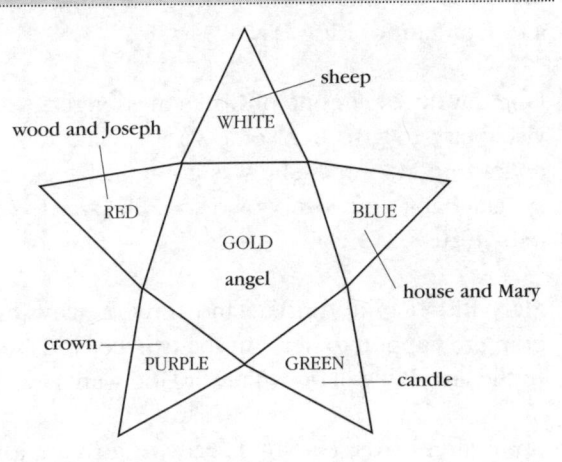

Star diagram with labels:
- WHITE — sheep
- RED — wood and Joseph
- BLUE — house and Mary
- PURPLE — crown
- GREEN — candle
- GOLD — angel

The segments join together to create a five-point star. Each segment tells a different part of the story.

OPENING ACTIVITY

As the children arrive, invite them to join the circle. Begin by asking the children to think about something that is very special to them—maybe something they own, a special place or person or even a special memory. After allowing time for the children to respond, lay the gold-coloured pentagon on the floor in front of you.

I wonder what this could be?	→ Reflect on the colour gold. Things made out of gold are often precious or special.
I wonder what else there is in the box (or basket)?	→ Introduce the white triangle and begin to tell the story.
Remember how the prophet Isaiah told the people of Israel that one day God was going to send them a great king, a Messiah who would come and rescue them. The Messiah would rescue them from all that was wrong and that made the world an unhappy place.	→ Place one of the sheep from Advent 2 on the triangle.
Many years later, that promise began to come true. In a little town called Nazareth lived a young teenage girl called Mary. She loved God and was faithful to him. She knew the stories of all that he had done, and the promise that one day he would send a special king, the Messiah.	→ Place the blue triangle next to the white and add the small flat-roofed house. Add the figure of Mary.
Mary was engaged to be married to a young carpenter called Joseph. There was always something for the carpenter in the town to mend—doors, ladders, the wheels on a cart—so Joseph was kept busy.	→ Place the red triangle, on the other side of the white triangle. Add something made from wood and the figure of Joseph.
Joseph's family could trace their history all the way back to King David—one of the good and faithful kings of long ago. This family link Joseph had with King David was to be important, as God had promised that the Messiah, the great king, would be a descendant of King David.	→ Place the purple triangle next to the red triangle. Place a crown or crown shape on the triangle.
One day an angel, one of God's messengers, came to visit Mary to give her some very special news. The angel told Mary that she was going to have a baby, a special baby, God's very own son. She was to call the baby Jesus.	→ Now point to the centre shape—the gold pentagon. Place the figure of the angel in the centre.
Mary didn't quite understand how or why this was going to happen to her, but she trusted God, and said to the angel, 'I will do whatever God wants me to do.'	→ Move the figure of Mary from the blue triangle into the centre shape.
Soon afterwards, Mary got ready to go on a journey. She was going to visit her cousin Elizabeth because the angel had told her that Elizabeth was also going to have a baby. Elizabeth lived in another town in the hills and Mary set off to tell her the special news.	→ Complete the star by adding the green triangle. Move Mary into the green triangle.
As Mary entered Elizabeth's house and said hello, the baby growing inside Elizabeth wriggled with joy. Elizabeth was so excited that she hugged Mary, for she recognized that Mary really was going to be the mother of God's son.	→ Place a tealight candle in the triangle. Slowly light the candle.

WONDERING

- I wonder which part of the story you liked the best?
- I wonder what Mary really felt about the news?
- I wonder which part of the story is the most important?

CRAFT ACTIVITY: A TALKING STAR

You will need:
- ★ A five-pointed star photocopied from template
- ★ Crayons or felt-tipped pens in the colours used in the story
- ★ Paper or thin card

1. Draw round the stencil shape on the paper or card.
2. Colour the five points of the triangle in the five different colours used in the story and colour the centre part of the star gold.
3. Cut out the star shape. Draw the symbols in each space to tell the story:

White: Woolly sheep
(the promised Messiah)

Blue: Flat-roofed house
(Mary lived in Nazareth)

Red: Rings
(Mary was engaged to Joseph)

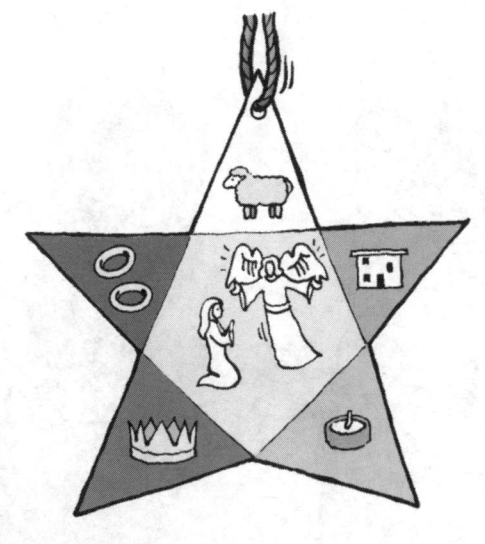

Purple: Crown
(Joseph was a descendant of King David)

Green: Candle
(Mary visits Elizabeth)

Gold centre: Figures of Mary and the angel
(The angel appeared to Mary)

4. Fold each triangle over, starting with the green triangle, then purple, red, blue and finally white. Now the children can retell the story by unfolding the triangles one section at a time, starting with the white triangle.
5. Alternatively, punch a hole in the top point of the star and thread some Christmas thread through the hole. Hang up as a Christmas talking star decoration.

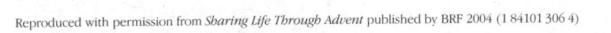

PICTURING THE BIBLE

Read Luke 1:26–28 and 39–45 and talk about the story. What special news Mary and Elizabeth had to tell each other! Elizabeth said, 'The Lord has blessed you because you believed that he will keep his promise' (Luke 1:45).

We know that the message came true and that Mary did have the baby and called him Jesus just as the angel had said. In a few days' time, it will be Christmas Day, when we celebrate Jesus' birthday.

CANDLE TIME

Light the candle in the clay lamp and together say, 'God's special promise has come true.'

Place the clay lamp on the floor in the middle of the circle.

Leader: God said, 'I have given you the freedom to choose.'

Light a tealight and place it in the middle of the circle.

All: God's promise has come true!

Leader: Isaiah told the people of Israel, 'Get ready to be rescued.'

Light a tealight and place it in the middle of the circle.

All: God's promise has come true!

Leader: John told the people the good news that God's new king was coming.

Light a tealight and place it in the middle of the circle.

All: God's promise has come true!

Leader: The angel told Mary, 'You are going to have a special baby—God's own son!'

Light a tealight and place it in the middle of the circle.

All: God's promise has come true!

Pause.

Leader: On the night that Jesus was born, the sky was full of stars. It was the stars that led the wise men from the East to where Jesus was born. We too are told to shine as stars in the world—passing on the good news of Jesus, God's very own son.

Pass round a pot containing little silver confetti stars. Invite the children to take a few stars each. When everyone has some stars, sprinkle some leftover stars around the tealights.

Pause. Invite the children to take their stars into church with them and give them to friends, family or members of the congregation. As each star is given, they should tell the recipient, 'God's promises have come true!'

SHARING LIFE THROUGH ADVENT WITH FAMILIES

INTRODUCTION

Christmas can be a season fraught with activity and busyness. We can often arrive at Christmas Day having forgotten what the real celebration is about. Here are some ideas for how the whole family can make the important countdown to Christmas more meaningful and exciting. At the heart of all celebrations there is a place for:

- Story
- Symbol
- Sharing
- Remembering and often resolution

In each of the four weeks of Advent, you will see these four themes recurring. You will be encouraged to discover the significance of colour, create your own family prayers, share stories, decorate the home, prepare special foods and maybe even have time to play a game or two.

Some families may set aside a time each day to light the candle and share the ideas, maybe during a shared meal. Other families may find it easier to set aside time just once a week. Either way, with the use of the four Bible passages, candle and suggestions for different family activities, you can do as little or as much as you choose, or as time allows.

So join in the Advent journey and follow us all the way to Bethlehem!

KEY TO ACTIVITIES

Light the candle

Thinking about the story

Themes to explore

Pray together

Things to make

Games to play

IDEAS FOR USING THE MATERIAL

- As a family, decide whether you are going to light the candle at the meal table, or whether you are going to set up a special focus space where the candle might be placed. This might be on a special table or shelf.
- Decide when you might share this special time together. It might be at a mealtime, at bedtime or even during the weekend.
- Use a modern version of the Bible for the readings.
- Involve different members of the family in reading the Bible passage.
- Don't be afraid to repeat the reading of the same passage over several days. Different things might come out of the passage with repeated reading.
- Encourage each member of the family to contribute to any conversation about the passage or the picture if they wish to, and really listen to each other.
- In some churches, the Christian festivals are marked by special liturgical colours. This might be picked up in the clothes worn by the minister or on altar frontals or cloths. The liturgical colour for Advent is purple. As a family, you might want to mark this special time by using a purple cloth or serviettes at the table. They might be paper cloths and serviettes, or the children might like to make special place-mats decorated in purple.
- Follow the instructions and make a Christmas garland to hang on your Christmas tree or in your house. Each week there will be ideas for adding a different symbol to your garland. The finished garland will tell the story of your journey through Advent.
- Where young children are involved, take special care with the lighting and positioning of the candle. Do not leave matches where children can reach them.

YEAR B

ADVENT 1

LIKE CLAY IN THE POTTER'S HAND

ISAIAH 64:1–9

Light the candle and read Isaiah 64:1–9. The people of Israel are feeling very sorry for themselves in today's reading. They are in exile in a strange land after their beautiful city of Jerusalem was taken from them. They know they have been ignoring God—turning their backs on him—but now they remember that God is their father and, like clay in the potter's hand, he could remould them and make everything right.

Think about the story together and talk about what the writer is saying.

- I wonder what shape the pot on the potter's wheel will be when it is finished?
- I wonder what shape and colour of pot you would like to be?

Give each member of the family a piece of paper and have some pens on the table. Now draw pot shapes of each other, saying why you've drawn what you've drawn. This is an opportunity to share what characteristics you value in each other.

If using the material daily, you could explore different themes on different days.

- **Images of God**: Today's reading gives us two different images of God—God the Father and God the potter. Talk about which images of God you like the best and why. What other images of God do you have?
- **Disobedience**: The people of Israel had been disobedient to God and now they were feeling pretty miserable. What does it feel like when, as a family, you upset one another? What do you do to make things feel better?
- **Making choices**: Talk together about how you make choices. They may be choices about the future, where to go on holiday, how to celebrate an event, buying presents, choices between right and wrong actions, sometimes even about choosing a friend.
- **Saying sorry**: The people of Israel had to say they were sorry to God. Talk together about the different ways we can say and show that we are sorry.

- **Advent**: Advent is a time of anticipation—of getting ready. The word Advent means 'coming' and is the time when we get ready to celebrate Jesus' birthday. Sometimes, in the busyness of buying presents, decorating the house and preparing food, we forget about the real meaning of Christmas. Talk together about how you will keep Jesus in the middle of your Christmas. This may be an opportunity to talk about how you will use *Sharing Life through Advent* together.

For this time of praying together, you will need a tube of Smarties or similar. Place the Smarties in a bowl. Pass the bowl round and in turn choose a colour of Smartie that makes you think of a characteristic of God. Tell the rest of the family, before eating your Smartie, what characteristic you have thought of.

Think about times in the week when you hurt one another. Say 'sorry' to one another by offering a Smartie to the person you have hurt. Hold hands and together say 'sorry' to God for the times you have turned your backs on him. Pray that you will find ways of keeping Jesus in the centre of your Christmas.

Make a nativity scene. Each week of Advent, the readings will give us a clue for the next piece of the nativity. Ensure that each week

Sharing life through Advent with families

Reproduced with permission from *Sharing Life through Advent* published by BRF 2004 (1 84101 306 4)

the characters are made to approximately the same size.

This week the reading talked about God being like a potter and us being like the clay. Start your nativity scene by making Mary, Joseph, the baby and a donkey out of clay. (Large families could make some extra clay animals to place in the stable so that everyone has a turn to make something.)

You will need:
- ★ Self-hardening clay
- ★ Cocktail sticks
- ★ Modelling tools

CLAY FIGURES

Make cone-shaped bodies out of clay, approximately 6cm high. Roll out a ball of clay for the head and secure with a cocktail stick. Roll worm-shaped pieces for hair and headbands. Roll out flat pieces of clay for cloaks and headdresses. Use modelling tools to add features such as faces, hair and beards.

CLAY ANIMALS

Make animal shapes in proportion to the figures. Strengthen legs with cocktail sticks. Use modelling tools to create wool and fur effects. Leave all figures overnight on a board to dry, following the manufacturer's instructions.

Think how you would create the picture of this story. You might like to buy some special crayons, pens or paints to use on your picture. When you've finished, mount the picture on some card so that you can stand or hang it up as part of your Christmas decorations. (Card from a cereal box is ideal.)

You could fasten a small tag on the back of the picture so that it can be hung on a length of ribbon. Each week, add another picture to the ribbon and hang them in a special place for everyone to see.

YEAR B

ADVENT 2

GET READY TO BE RESCUED!

ISAIAH 40:1–11

Light the candle and read Isaiah 40:1–11. Remember how the people of Israel were feeling very miserable because they had been taken from their homes in Jerusalem to a strange land called Babylon. They longed to go home. Then one of God's messengers, the prophet Isaiah, came to the people with some good news—they were going home! The passage says that, like a shepherd, God will gather up his people and take them home. Look again at the second part of verse 10. There is a special mention of how God will care for the mothers and the children.

Think about the story together and talk about what the writer is saying.

- Which is your favourite part of the story?
- I wonder if the sheep recognize the shepherd?
- Isaiah paints a picture with words of how God cares for the people, just like a shepherd cares for his sheep. I wonder what image you would choose if you were painting a picture of the story?

If using the material daily, you could explore different themes on different days.

- **Being in a fix!**: Remember together any times when a member of the family got stuck, lost or locked out or in. How did it feel? Now remember how they were rescued. How did that feel?
- **Moving home**: Talk about moving house. You may have experienced this but, if not, think about how it might feel. What would you miss? Now imagine how it would feel if, like the Israelites, you were forced to leave your home and you could only take with you what you could carry. How would that feel and what three things would you want to take with you?
- **Where is Babylon?**: Look on a Bible map (there may be one in the back of your Bible, or, if you have access to the Internet, look it up there). See if you can find Jerusalem. Now look for Babylon. The Israelites were a long way from home! Look on a modern map and see if you can still find Jerusalem.
- **City of peace**: Jerusalem means 'city of peace', but instead it has been the focus of much fighting throughout history. Even today fighting continues in some parts. In Advent we remember Jesus coming to earth as a tiny baby, but we also remember Jesus' promise that, one day, he will come again. On that day he will make all things new—no more fighting, no more tears. Talk together about places or situations you would like to see changed and made new.

- **The shepherd and his sheep**: Shepherds are often talked about in the Bible. Together look up these passages: Psalm 23; Luke 2:8–20; Luke 15:3–7; and John 10:14–15. In Israel today, the shepherds still look after their sheep on the hillsides just as they did in the time of Jesus. Talk together about what you think a good shepherd would need to be like.

If you have an atlas, lay it on the table, open at the map of the whole world. During the week you might like to watch the news or look in newspapers for those parts of the world where there is fighting, where people are fleeing from their homes, or where people are hungry. You or your church may already

Sharing life through Advent with families

Reproduced with permission from *Sharing Life through Advent* published by BRF 2004 (1 84101 306 4)

support a project overseas. If you have already made the shepherds, place a shepherd on each part of the world that you are concerned about and pray for that situation. Alternatively place a tealight in each place.

Make the shepherds ready to add to your nativity.

You will need:
★ Corks (one for each shepherd)
★ Cotton polystyrene balls approx. 20mm, or ping-pong balls (one for each shepherd)
★ Scraps of coloured paper or felt or fabric
★ Brown pipe cleaners
★ Scissors
★ Glue and pens
★ Cotton wool

1. Glue the ball to the cork and leave to dry. When dry, cover the cork with fabric or brown card.
2. Use templates to make and cut out hands and arms. Attach hands to arms and then attach arms to cork.
3. Draw features on to face. Cut out beard and add, or use small bits of cotton wool.
4. Attach headdress and glue into place. Glue thin ribbon around headdress to finish it off.
5. Cut and shape pipe cleaner into a crook shape. Attach to inside of shepherd's hands.
6. You could also make a sheep from pipe cleaners and cotton wool to put in the shepherd's arms or round his neck.

Think how you would create the picture of this story. You might like to buy some special crayons, pens or paints to use on your picture. When you've finished mount the picture on some card so that you can stand, or hang it up as part of your Christmas decorations.

You could hang the picture on the ribbon next to the picture you made for Advent 1.

YEAR B

ADVENT 3

SPREAD THE GOOD NEWS

ISAIAH 61:1–4; JOHN 1:6–8, 19–28

Light the candle and read together Isaiah 61:1–4. This is the good news the people of Israel had been waiting for. They were at last going home to rebuild the city of Jerusalem.

Now we are going to leap forward in time to the New Testament, to read about someone else who brought good news. It starts with a riddle! Read together John 1:6–8. Who was John talking about who was called 'the light'?

Now read verses 19–28. Just like the prophet Isaiah, John was telling the people to get ready—to stop doing what was wrong and to say sorry to God, because soon the Messiah was coming.

Think about the story together and talk about what the writer is saying.

If using the material daily, you could explore different themes on different days.

- **Good news**: Think back over the last year and remember all the good news you have heard. It might have been good news within the family, at school, or at church. Talk about any current good news.
- **Getting ready**: Some good news is followed by a time of getting ready, such as the news about a new baby, a wedding, or a party. Advent is also a time of getting ready to celebrate the birthday of Jesus. Make a list together of all that still needs to be done to get ready—presents still to buy and wrap up, food, party invitations and so on. You might also be thinking about putting up your Christmas decorations.
- **Getting ourselves ready**: Tell each other the kinds of things that make you feel special. It might be something someone says, something you do, something you wear or even a gift you've received. We can feel special on the outside, but how do we feel special on the inside? John tells the people how they need to get ready on the inside and say 'sorry' for those things that they have done wrong.
- **Baptism**: John baptized the people as a sign of their saying sorry. Remember any baptisms you have been to. They may have been the baptisms of members of the family. Look out any photographs to remind you of the special day.
- **Light of the world**: Jesus is often called the light of the world. I wonder what that means to you? I wonder what it means when we are told to be light in the world as well? What Christmas lights will you be putting up this year? Let them remind you of Jesus the light of the world at the centre of your Christmas.

Jesus told us to be like lights in the world and to care for one another just as he did. Take a piece of A4 paper or similar. Fold it in half lengthwise and cut it in half.

Fold the paper backwards and forwards about four times like a concertina. On the front fold draw a person, making the hands and feet touch the folds of the paper. Now carefully cut the shape out, being careful not to cut through the folds at the hands and feet. Open out the paper and you should have a line of people holding hands.

Think together about people you know who are sad, unwell or lonely at this time and write their names or draw their faces on each of the paper people. Pray for them together. You might want to pin your paper people up somewhere where you can remember to pray for them each day.

Sharing life through Advent with families

GET THE STABLE READY

You will need:
- Shoe box or similar
- Straw or drinking straws
- Dark blue and yellow or brown paint or paper
- Silver paper and card
- Glue or double-sided tape
- Scissors

1. Take the lid off the shoe box and put it to one side. Paint the inside of the box brown or cover it with paper. Paint three of the outside sides of the box dark blue. (The bottom and back of the box can be left unpainted.)
2. Cut both short and one long sides off the box lid. Attach the lid to the bottom front of the box to create an extension to the floor of the stable.
3. Cut lengths of straw about half the height of the box and glue them around the inside of the box. Glue fine or chopped straw to the floor of the stable in a more random way. (Alternatively, use drinking straws and paint them a straw colour.)
4. Cut a star shape out of silver card, or cover white card with foil. (See template on page 29.) Attach a thin rectangle of card to the back of the star and fasten this to the back of the stable so that the star shows above the stable. Now add the figures to the stable.

Think how you would create the picture of this story. You might like to buy some special crayons, pens or paints to use on your picture. When you've finished, mount the picture on some card so that you can stand, or hang it up as part of your Christmas decorations.

You could hang the picture on the ribbon next to the pictures you made for Advent 1 and 2.

YEAR B

ADVENT 4

SOME VERY SPECIAL NEWS

LUKE 1:26–38 AND 39–45

Light the candle and read Luke 1:26–38. The time has come for God to fulfil his promise, and he sends his special angel messenger to the town of Nazareth to the home of a young teenage girl called Mary. The angel has some very special news for Mary.

Think about the story together and talk about what the writer is saying.

If using the material daily, you could explore different themes on different days.

- **Angels**: Look at the Christmas cards you have already received and pick out the ones with angels on them. Talk together about the different images of angels. What do you think they really look like? Look at Hebrews 13:2 and see what it says there about angels!
- **Mary says 'yes'**: I wonder what would have happened if Mary had said 'no' or made excuses to God? Look up these other famous Bible characters and see what they said when God asked them to do something great: Moses (Exodus 3:10, 11); Gideon (Judges 6:11–13a, 17); Zechariah (Luke 1:11–13, 18).
- **His name will be Jesus**: Do you know why you were given your name? What do you like about your name? What do you dislike? If you could change your name, what would you call yourself? The angel told Mary to call her baby Jesus.
- **Expecting a baby**: Look together at family baby pictures and see if you can recognize yourself and one another. Play the memory shopping game and think about all the things you need to get ready for a new baby: the first person starts, 'I went shopping and I bought some nappies.' The second person continues, 'I went shopping and bought some nappies and a big cuddly toy.' Carry on the game with each person repeating the list and adding a new item. With younger children you could draw the items like a shopping list.
- **Some very special news**: Think about hearing some very special news. Who would you want to tell about it? Not everyone remembers that Christmas is Jesus' birthday. Think if you have a friend or neighbour who wouldn't normally go to church. Perhaps you could invite them to go with you to one of the special Christmas services. Invite them into your home first for a drink and special Christmas biscuits.

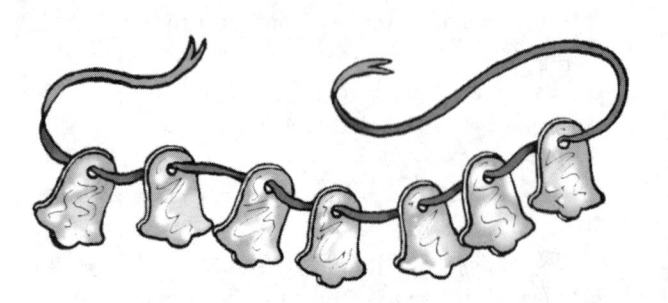

Over the centuries, church bells have been used to ring out messages of good news. Cut out some bell shapes from silver or gold card. On the back of each card write or draw something that you would like to say 'thank you' to God for. Join the prayers together with ribbon or thread and hang them on your Christmas tree.

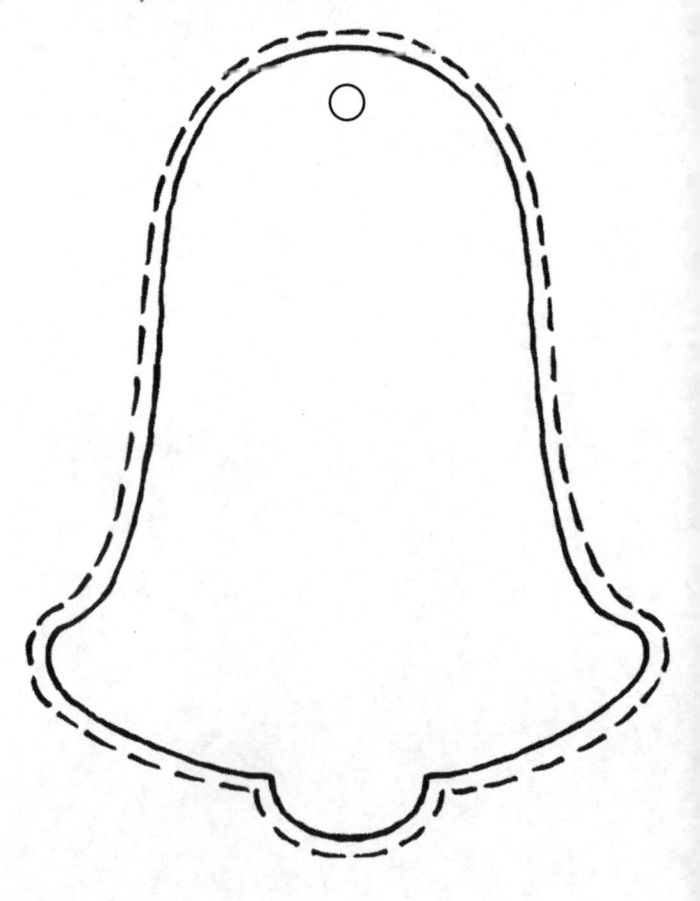

Sharing life through Advent with families

YEAR B

ANGELS BRING SPECIAL NEWS

You will need:
- Thin white card
- Ping-pong or polystyrene ball
- Glitter
- Tinsel strips
- Silver stars
- Small paper doily
- Scissors and glue

1. Cut a circle of card and make a slit to the centre. Wrap the card round to create a cone shape and stick the edge down.
2. Make two tiny slits in the front and push through a narrow strip of card for arms. Cut a hand shape at each end.
3. Mark features on the ping-pong or polystyrene ball and make a small hole in the base.
4. Stick head to cone shape. Add silver tinsel strips to the head.
5. Cut the doily into four. Carefully make folds in the doily at the pointed end and stick two sections to the back of the angel. Put glue on the edge of the doily wings and bottom of the angel dress and sprinkle with silver glitter. Leave to dry before adding to your nativity scene.

CHRISTMAS BISCUITS FOR YOUR GUESTS

You will need:
- 150g plain flour
- 25g cornflour
- 75g margarine
- 40g caster sugar
- 1/2 tsp vanilla essence
- 1 egg white
- 2 tbsp milk

For decoration:
- 2 tbsp apricot glaze
- 500g ready-to-roll icing
- Coloured dragees
- Food colouring or icing pens
- 1 metre ribbon (2.5mm width) if hanging from tree

1. Sift flour and cornflour into bowl and rub in margarine until it looks like breadcrumbs.
2. Stir in remaining ingredients and mix to a firm dough. Knead on floured board until smooth.
3. Roll out dough thinly and, using cutters, cut square, round and heart shapes.
4. Place shapes on baking sheet. Use a drinking straw to make a hole in the top of each for hanging on the tree.
5. Bake in a preheated oven at 180°C/350°F/Gas Mark 4 for 10–15 minutes. Cool on wire rack.
6. Roll out icing and cut to same shape as biscuits. Brush apricot glaze on cooled biscuits and gently press icing on top.
7. Decorate with dragees, coloured icing shapes or icing pens. Press hole through icing and thread with ribbon to hang on tree.

Think how you would create the picture of this story. You might like to buy some special crayons, pens or paints to use on your picture. When you've finished, mount the picture on some card so that you can stand or hang it up as part of your Christmas decorations.

You could complete your line of pictures by hanging this one on the ribbon with the others you have made.

Sharing life through Advent with families

SHARING LIFE THROUGH ADVENT BIBLE READING NOTES

YEAR B

ADVENT 1

LIKE CLAY IN THE POTTER'S HAND

ISAIAH 64:1–9

KEY VERSE

You, Lord, are our Father. We are nothing but clay, but you are the potter who moulded us.
ISAIAH 64:8

This is an image often used in the Bible to describe the relationship between us and our Creator—clay in the hands of the master potter. It probably goes back to the story in Genesis 2 of the creation of Adam, when the Lord God 'took a handful of soil and made a man' (v. 7). The one who originally shaped us from the dust of the ground is the one who can reshape us when it is necessary.

The picture here is of us human beings as clay pots, spoilt by the sins that cause God to turn his back on us. We need to be remade, and only the potter who originally made us can do it. Flawed, we need 'the potter who moulded us' to take the clay and reshape it, removing all the faults and damage caused by disobedience.

In today's society we may not be very familiar with the skill of the potter, sitting at the wheel and using just his two hands gently to mould the pot. Perhaps, for some of us, the skill of the panel beater in the car repair workshop is more relevant! In both cases, damage is being repaired and the object brought back to its original shape and value.

It's a very positive thought that no matter how damaged and disfigured the vessel or the vehicle, it can be restored. But of course first we have to acknowledge the damage, and then trust the 'repairer' to do his work. Admitting that we have failed God and fallen short of his standards is the first step. Recognizing that we not capable of putting things right ourselves is the second. Believing that God is able to remake and restore us is the third.

TO THINK ABOUT

Each step in the process of spiritual 'repair' is captured in this picture of the potter at his wheel. He picks up the apparently useless and flawed lump of clay, and then makes something useful and beautiful out of it.

A PRAYER

Master potter, who at the first shaped us and made us, help us to recognize the failures and sins that have spoilt your work. 'Only by your help can we ever be saved.' We trust you to take the unpromising material of our lives and reshape it to a new beauty and usefulness. Amen

YEAR B

ADVENT 2

GET READY TO BE RESCUED!

ISAIAH 40:1–11

KEY VERSE

The Lord cares for his nation, just as shepherds care for their flocks.
ISAIAH 40:11

TO THINK ABOUT

Here in this picture of the conquering saviour and the good shepherd we can see two sides to God's character—infinite power, which we would be foolish to forget, and infinite love, which we would be foolish to reject.

A PRAYER

Lord God, help us to prepare for you to come to us by recognizing your power and your love, both of which, in their different ways, are irresistible.

These words were addressed to the people of Judah, and especially the city of Jerusalem. Many of them had been exiles in Babylon, following the fall of Jerusalem to the invaders over 60 years earlier. Perhaps they had lost hope of ever again seeing their native land and their homes. But now the voice of the prophet rings out in the street, not with the usual words of warning and judgment, but of comfort and hope: 'Your slavery is past; your punishment is over' (v. 2). The Lord is about to come to them in a new way. They were to shout it from the hilltops: 'Your God is here!' (v. 9).

To the people of Judah it was the Babylonians who had seemed all-powerful, but now they were reminded dramatically that it is the Lord God who has the 'mighty arm'—and he is coming to their rescue. So they must get ready for his arrival. There are things to be done—paths to be cleared, rough and rugged ground to be levelled, so that God's pathway is open. The language is not literal, of course: they could hardly be expected to flatten the hills on which the city stands! But it reminds the waiting people that they have a part to play in their own salvation. They can level the 'rough places' in their own lives and open a way for the Lord to enter.

The final picture is a very beautiful one. The powerful Lord God does not come simply as an avenging conqueror, but as a gentle shepherd to his flock. He cares for them in the same way as a shepherd cares for his sheep, leading the ones who are able to walk and carrying the ones who are too small and weak even to do that.

YEAR B

ADVENT 3

SPREAD THE GOOD NEWS

ISAIAH 61:1–4, 8–11; JOHN 1:6–8, 19–28

KEY VERSE

I am only someone shouting in the desert, 'Get the road ready for the Lord!'
JOHN 1:23

TO THINK ABOUT

Voices can spread good news, but if nobody listens to them and acts on what they say, they might as well keep silent. It's one thing to believe that God speaks to us—through the Bible, through preaching, through prayer, through friends, through circumstances. It's quite another to hear what he says and try to act on it. Without our response, the good news can never be spread.

A PRAYER

Lord, help us to listen to your voice and be ready to do what you say. May we never ignore your message of hope, but be prepared to hear and receive the good news, and then pass it on to others who have not heard it.

Voices are fascinating things—familiar and friendly, cold and menacing, soft and loud. We love to hear a friendly voice but, from childhood, we shrink from an angry one. Both the Old Testament passage (which is the prophet describing how the Spirit of God has empowered him to tell good news to the people) and the reading from John's Gospel (which is all about John the Baptist) are basically about voices, and the things they say.

John the Baptist was a very important figure in his time, attracting huge crowds from Jerusalem and the surrounding areas to hear him as he called out his message in the Jordan valley, and to be baptized by him in the river. Yet he liked to play down his role. 'Me? I'm just a messenger,' he would say. True, but he was no less than the long-promised 'voice' who would call on people to get ready for the coming of the Messiah, God's deliverer. John's message was much the same as Isaiah's: 'The Lord is coming to bless and save his people—so, be ready for him!'

The problem, in both cases, was much the same. How would they know when all this was happening? Supposing they missed the coming of the Lord? John warned them of the danger. 'Here with you is someone you don't know!' And that 'someone' would be the one God had promised, who would not simply baptize with water, like John, for cleansing and a new start, but inwardly and powerfully with the Holy Spirit. John saw his role as simply to point out this 'unknown Saviour', spread the good news of his coming, and then slip quietly away.

Sharing life through Advent Bible reading notes

YEAR B

ADVENT 4

SOME VERY SPECIAL NEWS

LUKE 1:26–38 AND 39–45

KEY VERSE

Mary said, 'I am the Lord's servant! Let it happen as you have said.'
LUKE 1:38

TO THINK ABOUT

The good news that we hear every year at Christmas may not seem as awesome as the very special news that Mary heard from the voice of the angel, but it also carries a responsibility and asks for a response. Will I accept it? Will I believe it? And will I—as Mary immediately did with her cousin Elizabeth—share it with others?

A PRAYER

Lord, help us, when we hear the familiar words of the Gospel at Christmas, to say 'yes' to the very special news that you have for each one of us, rather than a hesitant 'maybe' or a cautious 'not yet'.

In just a few moments, the life of a teenage girl in Nazareth was changed for ever. Before, she was going to marry the village carpenter—in fact, she was engaged to him. Then, she would have assumed, would follow the birth of their children and the domestic life of a first-century Jewish home—cooking, washing, teaching the children, Friday prayers and synagogue on the Sabbath.

But once the angel had brought this very special news, the picture changed beyond recognition. She would be the mother of the Messiah, that was what the angel had said—the dream of every Jewish woman. What she couldn't possibly have foreseen were all the other things—the joy and suffering, the bereavement and then the resurrection, the day of Pentecost and all that followed. And beyond that, right through Christian history, to be the 'truly blessed' one, the one with whom God was 'pleased', honoured and revered wherever the Christian faith is believed.

Yet Mary had a choice, it would seem. 'Nothing is impossible for God' (v. 37), but when he chooses human instruments for his purpose they don't stop being human—which means they can say 'no'. Mary's agreement was required—her willing acceptance of this calling, so awesome and so unexpected. There are no conscripts in God's army, only volunteers.

Yet her response seems to have been immediate. 'I am the Lord's servant!' That wasn't just an instant reaction, but a response shaped by this young girl's deep and genuine faith. 'Let it happen as you have said.'

Sharing life through Advent Bible reading notes

SHARING LIFE THROUGH COLLECTIVE WORSHIP

ADVENT 1: LIKE CLAY IN THE POTTER'S HAND

ISAIAH 64:1–9

INTRODUCTION

This first assembly reminds children that we are moving into the season called Advent when we remember how much God cares about us.

FOCUS

The focus is a low table covered with a purple cloth. In the centre of the table, place a large candle. Place some clay and/or pots made out of clay around the candle.

Welcome the children and ask them if they know what time of year it is. Explain that Advent is the time when the Christian Church gets ready to celebrate the birthday of Jesus on Christmas Day. The purple cloth is the colour for getting ready and the candle reminds us that Jesus was often called the light of the world.

The birth of Jesus was just part of God's story of love but it wasn't the beginning, so in this assembly we are going right back to the very beginning of God's story. Explain to the children how, right at the very beginning, God made the world and everything that is in it. God took some soil from the ground... *(at this point the leader takes some clay from the table and begins to mould it into a person shape)* ... and breathed life into it *(pretend to breath life into the clay shape)*.

Invite a child to read Genesis 2:7: 'The Lord God took a handful of soil and made a man. God breathed life into the man, and the man started breathing.'

Wonder with the children how God might have felt. God told people how to live happily together, to care for one another and not to hurt one another, but it wasn't long before the people stopped listening to God.

Many, many years later, the people of Israel were feeling very sorry for themselves. They had been taken prisoners from their beautiful city called Jerusalem to a strange land. They were like refugees, in a place they didn't want to be, and they couldn't go home. They were very sad, and they prayed to God to help them.

The people of Israel said that they were like useless clay, but that God was like a potter who had made them and shaped them, and could make them good and useful again. They remembered that God was like the very best kind of father and so they prayed to God for help.

Read these words from Isaiah 64:8–9:

> *You, Lord, are our Father. We are nothing but clay, but you are the potter who moulded us. Don't be so furious or keep our sins in your thoughts for ever! Remember that all of us are your people.*

Invite the children to identify elements of the story that reflect what the people of Israel were saying.

- How does it feel when you know you have been disobedient?
- What does it feel like when you have fallen out with your friends?
- What does it feel like when you get into trouble?
- What do you do to make things better?

REFLECTION

The people of Israel knew they had been disobedient, and now they wanted to say 'sorry' to God. When we do things wrong we need to say 'sorry' too. First, we need to say 'sorry' to the person we have hurt or upset and then we need to say 'sorry' to God. When we hurt one another, we also make God sad.

Light the candle on the focus table and remind the children that:

- Jesus came to be the light of the world.
- Jesus came to show us how to live caring for one another.

Invite the children to think about anything they have done today where they haven't cared for one another and where instead they have hurt someone.

PRAYER

Father God, we are sorry when we get things wrong and hurt others. Please help us to care for one another in school, in the playground, at home, and wherever we are. Amen

SONGS

Make me a channel of your peace
Spirit of God, unseen as the wind

FOLLOW-ON WORK

Talk about the effects of being disobedient. Talk about making choices. How do you decide between good choices and bad choices? Invite the children to make their own models using clay, thinking about how God modelled us from the soil of the earth.

✵

ADVENT 2: GET READY TO BE RESCUED!

ISAIAH 40:1–11

INTRODUCTION

This assembly looks at what it feels like to be rescued and thinks about people today who are refugees.

FOCUS

The focus is a low table covered with a purple cloth. In the centre of the table, place a large candle. Place a globe or a map of the world, and a shepherd with his sheep, around the candle.

Welcome the children and ask if any of them have ever got locked in somewhere, or lost, or stuck up a tree. Ask how they were rescued. What did it feel like to be stuck? What did it feel like to be rescued?

Remind the children that last week they heard about how the people of Israel were taken prisoners and sent to a strange land. Look on the globe or a map and show the children where Jerusalem is. Babylon, the place where the people were sent, was a long way away, across a desert. The people of Israel longed to go home and they had prayed to God. Then, one day, one of God's messengers, whom the people called a prophet, came to them with some good news: they were going home!

Read Isaiah 40:1–2a and 11.

> *Our God has said: 'Encourage my people! Give them comfort. Speak kindly to Jerusalem and announce: Your slavery is past...' The Lord cares for his nation, just as shepherds care for their flocks. He carries the lambs in his arms, while gently leading the mother sheep.*

Ask the children if they remember how God was described last week. God was called 'father' and described as a potter. This week, the prophet Isaiah paints a picture of God in words. Ask the children:

- Which is your favourite part of the story?
- What picture would you draw to show what God is like?

God promised the people that they were going home to Jerusalem. Their time as refugees was over and it was time to go home and rebuild their city. I wonder how the people of Israel felt when they heard the news?

REFLECTION

There are still people in the world today who, like the people of Israel, have been driven from their homes because of fighting—families who leave behind everything they own and move to a new land. Look again at the map of the world, or the globe, and identify places where this might be happening. You might have some newspaper cuttings or photographs that you could show the children at this point.

Place the pictures where the children can see them and light the Advent candle. Remind the children that Jesus came to be the light of the world, to show people how to live at peace with one another. Still today people hurt one another by saying unkind things, by fighting and by not sharing with each other.

PRAYER

Dear Lord Jesus, we pray for those parts of the world where there is fighting and where people have to leave their homes. We pray for refugees all over the world who long to go home and live in peace.

SONGS

Cross over the road
When I needed a neighbour
Peace perfect peace

FOLLOW-ON WORK

Talk together about refugees in today's world. Look through newspapers and magazines for pictures of refugees or people fighting. Make a collage or poster of the pictures and use it as a special prayer focus for the week. Talk together about what it would be like to have to leave everything behind and go to live in a strange land.

ADVENT 3: SPREAD THE GOOD NEWS

ISAIAH 61:1–4, 8–11; JOHN 1:6–8, 19–28

INTRODUCTION

This assembly will look at how we get ourselves ready to celebrate the birthday of Jesus.

FOCUS

The focus is a low table covered with a purple cloth, with the Advent candle in the centre.

Welcome the children and tell them that you have got some really good news for them. Suggest one or two pieces of good news that won't really interest the children—for example, your favourite football team (some obscure team) won its football match at the weekend. Sensing the children's lack of enthusiasm for your good news, ask them if they have any good news to tell you. You might finish with the good news that there are only 'xx' days left until school breaks up for Christmas.

Remind the children that last week we learnt how the people of Israel received some good news from the prophet Isaiah. They were told that, at last, their time as refugees was over and that they were going home!

Today we hear about another of God's prophets, a man called John, who many years later brought some more good news to the people in Jerusalem. John seemed to be talking in riddles, but see if you can work out whom he is talking about.

Read John 1:6–8:

> *God sent a man named John, who came to tell about the light and to lead all people to have faith. John wasn't that light. He came only to tell about the light. The true light that shines on everyone was coming into the world.*

Allow time for the children to try to solve the riddle. Remind the children of the candle on the Advent focus table. The candle reminds us that Jesus was sometimes called the light of the world. The people asked John if he was the promised new king—the Messiah whom God had promised to send into the world. But John said he was just bringing the good news that the new king was coming, and that the people should get themselves ready to welcome him.

John told the people to get ready for the coming Messiah, to say they were sorry for the things they were doing wrong. John baptized the people in the river as a sign that they were forgiven.

Invite the children's responses to this story. Ask if any of the children present have been baptized. How was their baptism different from the way that John baptized people?

Explain that today, when people are baptized in church, they are given a candle to remind them that Jesus is the light of the world who shows us the way to live.

REFLECTION

John came to tell the people the good news that the Messiah—the new king—was coming and that they needed to get ready to meet him. Advent is the time when we get ready to celebrate Jesus the Messiah being born. We too need to get ready, but sometimes we are so busy putting up decorations and thinking about what presents we might get that we forget what Christmas is really about.

Light the Advent candle and play a piece of quiet music. Invite the children to think about how they will remember Jesus this Christmas. They might think about Jesus when they look at the lights on the Christmas tree or the candles on the table on Christmas Day. These things remind us that Jesus is the light of the world who shows us how to care for one another.

PRAYER

Father God, thank you that you kept your promise to send Jesus into the world to show us how to live in peace with one another. Help us, like Jesus, to shine as lights in the world in all we do and say.

SONGS

This little light of mine
Give me oil in my lamp
Go tell it on the mountain

FOLLOW-ON WORK

Talk about how we get ready to welcome somebody special. What needs to be done to get ready for Christmas? Talk about what it means that Jesus is the light of the world. Make Christmas cards showing Jesus to be the light of the world.

✱

ADVENT 4: SOME VERY SPECIAL NEWS

LUKE 1:26–38 AND 39–45

INTRODUCTION

This assembly tells the story of the angel's visit to Mary and how we continue to celebrate the good news of Jesus' birth.

FOCUS

The focus is a low table covered with a purple cloth. Place the Advent candle in the centre of the table. You will also need the following items, which can be added to the focus by different children as the assembly unfolds:

- A sheep
- Nativity figures of Mary, Joseph and the angel
- Something made from wood
- A small crown

Welcome the children and remind them that today is the last week of Advent and that it is only 'xx' days until Christmas Day, when we remember God sent his son Jesus into the world. Use the script to tell the story of how Mary received some very special news.

Remember how the prophet Isaiah told the people of Israel that one day God was going to send them a great king, a Messiah who would come and rescue them. The Messiah would rescue them from all that was wrong and that made the world an unhappy place.	→ Place one of the sheep on the table.
Many years later, that promise began to come true. In a little town called Nazareth lived a young teenage girl called Mary. She loved God and was faithful to him. She knew the stories of all that he had done, and the promise that one day he would send a special king, the Messiah.	→ Place the figure of Mary on the table.
Mary was engaged to be married to a young carpenter called Joseph. There was always something for the carpenter in the town to mend: doors, ladders, cartwheels… so Joseph was kept very busy.	→ Add something made from wood and the figure of Joseph.
Joseph's family could trace their history all the way back to King David—one of the good and faithful kings of long ago. Joseph's family link with King David was to be important, as God promised that the Messiah, the great king, would be a descendant of King David.	→ Place the small crown on the table.
One day, an angel, one of God's messengers, came to visit Mary to give her some very special news. The angel told Mary that she was going to have a baby—a special baby, God's very own son. She was to call the baby Jesus. Mary didn't quite understand how or why this was going to happen to her, but she trusted God, and said to the angel, 'I will do whatever God wants me to do.'	→ Place the figure of the angel next to Mary.
Soon afterwards, Mary got ready to go on a journey. She was going to visit her cousin Elizabeth because the angel had told her that Elizabeth was also going to have a baby. Elizabeth lived in another town in the hills and Mary set off to tell her the special news. As Mary entered Elizabeth's house and said hello, the baby growing inside Elizabeth wriggled with joy. Elizabeth was so excited that she hugged Mary, for she recognized that Mary really was going to be the mother of God's son.	→ Pick Mary up off the table and hold her for the children to see. Place Mary back on the table. Slowly light the Advent candle.
	Pause.

Reproduced with permission from *Sharing Life through Advent* published by BRF 2004 (1 84101 306 4)

Invite the children to talk about the events of the story. Think about what you would do if you had some very special news. Who would be the first person that you would want to go and share it with?

REFLECTION

God promised that one day he would send his son into the world to tell the people how much he loved them and to show them how to care for one another. The people waited many years to see God fulfil his promise. Today, over 2000 years later, we still remember that special time when the angels announced that Jesus was born.

Point to the lit Advent candle and remind the children that Jesus is the light of the world.

PRAYER

Dear Lord Jesus, thank you that you came to earth as a tiny baby. Thank you that when you grew up, you taught us ways to care for one another. Help us to pass on the message of your love as we care for one another.

SONGS

Mary had a baby, yes, Lord
It was on a starry night

FOLLOW-ON WORK

Mary was told to call her baby Jesus, which means 'Emmanuel' or 'God with us'. Ask the children if they know why they were given their names and find out together what their names mean.

Talk about angels and how, over the years, different artists have painted them. Ask the children what they think an angel might look like. Invite the children to paint or draw their ideas.

★ ★ ★ YEAR C ★ ★ ★

COMING

SHARING LIFE THROUGH WORSHIP

INTRODUCTION

Advent is a time of anticipation, preparation and waiting. It's a time in the Church's calendar when we prepare once again to celebrate the birth of Jesus the promised Messiah. This Advent, through the weekly readings, we will explore the word Advent which means 'coming'. Here we will also see echoed those three words: anticipation, preparation and waiting.

Through the prophets Jeremiah and Malachi, we will see the people of Israel *anticipating* the coming of the promised Messiah. John the Baptist tells the people to *prepare* themselves for the *coming* of the Messiah, and Jesus tells us to watch and *wait* for the time when he will *come* again in glory to redeem the world. So Advent is about the past, the present and the future. The past points to the promises of God to the people of Israel, fulfilled in the birth of Jesus. The present is our preparation for celebrating Jesus' birth, and the future is informed by all that Jesus taught us about bringing his kingdom in the world until he comes again — our future hope!

This introduction includes some ideas and liturgical responses for use during the four weeks of Advent. They are based around the lighting of the four Advent candles. The lighting of the Advent candles may differ according to local situations, and may depend on when the children are present in the service. The material can be used either with an adult congregation or with an all-age congregation. In those churches where there is not a service every week in the same church building, the Advent wreath and accompanying symbols could be taken from one church in the group, circuit or benefice to the next. (For instructions on how to make an Advent wreath, see page 80.)

LIGHTING THE ADVENT CANDLES DURING SUNDAY WORSHIP

If the children are present at the beginning of the service, they could share in the lighting of the Advent candle. After this they might go off into their groups during the singing of an appropriate hymn to continue using the children's material. If, however, the children come in towards the end of the service, the lighting of the Advent candles may be kept until they are present. The children could then be invited to participate. Following the lighting of the Advent candle, members of the congregation could be encouraged to take the light out with them into the rest of the week by using the materials offered in 'Sharing life through Advent with families' (see pages 89–97).

The suggested pattern for each week is as follows:

- The Advent wreath is placed on a stand where all can see it, with a smaller table beside it.
- For Advent 1, 2 and 3, a member of the congregation comes forward dressed as a prophet and delivers God's word to the people (script starts on page 77). In Advent 4 the characters will be Mary and Elizabeth.
- A child or young person, who carries the symbol for the week, accompanies each speaker.
- After the reading, the reader takes the symbol from the child, holds it up and then places it on the table using the words given.
- The child or young person is then invited to light the Advent candle or candles.
- Allow a few moments for quiet reflection.
- The prayer given in the liturgical notes could then be said either by the young person or the whole congregation.

SYMBOLS

Advent 1   Crown (made from card or purchased from a party shop)
Advent 2   Scroll, and silver and gold coins (chocolate pennies)
Advent 3   Baptism jug of water and bowl
Advent 4   Words of the Magnificat written on card

SHARING LIFE THROUGH ADVENT WITH THE WHOLE CONGREGATION

Have prepared an Advent wreath with five candles. Three of the candles might be purple, the liturgical colour for Advent; one pink for Advent 3, Gaudete Sunday (for information about this, see 'Sharing life through Advent with children' page 84); and white in the centre for Christmas Day.

Place the Advent wreath on a stand so that it is visible to the whole congregation. You could place it on a long drape of purple fabric so that the symbols for each week can be placed at its base. Alternatively, place a small table covered with a cloth next to the stand to place the symbols on.

Invite members of the congregation (three men and two women) to prepare the readings for the four weeks of Advent and to wear appropriate clothing, or, if desired, simply to represent their character by use of a headdress. These five people will bring the symbol for the week and God's word to the people during the lighting of the Advent candle.

ADVENT 1: SPOTTING THE SIGNS

JEREMIAH 33:14–16; LUKE 21:25–36

The first reader walks forward, accompanied by a child who carries the crown symbol.

First reader

I am the prophet Jeremiah and the Lord has sent me to tell you: 'I made a wonderful promise to Israel and Judah, and the days are coming when I will keep it. I promise that the time will come when I will appoint a king from the family of David, a king who will be honest and rule with justice. In those days, Judah will be safe; Jerusalem will have peace and will be named, "The Lord Gives Justice".'
JEREMIAH 33:14–16

The child passes the crown to the reader, who holds it up for all to see and says:

I bring a crown—the symbol of God's promise that a king is coming who will rule the world with justice.

The reader places the crown on the table, or at the base of the Advent candle.
The child lights the first of the Advent candles.

Prayer for the week

You teach us, Lord, to look for the signs of the coming of your kingdom. Teach us also how to pray for its dawning.

ADVENT 2: GETTING OURSELVES READY

MALACHI 3:1–4; LUKE 3:1–6

The second reader walks forward, accompanied by a child who carries a scroll and silver or gold coins.

Second reader

I am the prophet Malachi and the Lord has sent me to tell you: 'I, the Lord All-Powerful, will send my messenger to prepare the way for me. Then suddenly the Lord you are looking for will appear in his temple. The messenger you desire is coming with my promise, and he is on his way. On the day the Lord comes, he will be like a furnace that purifies silver or like strong soap in a washbasin. No one will be able to stand up to him. The Lord will purify the descendants of Levi, as though they were gold or silver. Then they will bring the proper offerings to the Lord, and the offerings of the people of Judah and Jerusalem will please him, just as they did in the past.'
MALACHI 3:1–4

The child passes the scroll and coins to the reader, who holds them up for all to see and says:

I bring a scroll that is written with God's words—that a messenger is coming who will prepare the way for the Lord—and gold and silver coins to show that he will purify his people.

The reader places the scroll and the coins on the table with the crown, or at the base of the Advent candle.
The child lights the first and second Advent candles.

Prayer for the week

Search our hearts, gracious God, and show us if there is anything impure or harmful there, so that we may repent of our sins, know your forgiveness and be ready to welcome you when you come.

ADVENT 3: BE JOYFUL

ZEPHANIAH 3:14–20; LUKE 3:7–18

The third reader walks forward, accompanied by a child who carries the symbol of water.

Third reader

I am John the Baptist and the Lord has sent me to tell you: 'Turn back to God and be baptized! Then your sins will be forgiven.' (Pause.)

Verses 7–15 could be read using other voices in the congregation and a narrator. Alternatively, the third reader moves straight to verse 16.

'I am just baptizing with water. But someone more powerful is going to come, and I am not good enough even to untie his sandals. He will baptize you with the Holy Spirit and with fire.'
LUKE 3:16

The child passes the jug of water to the reader, who holds it up for all to see and says:

I bring water, the symbol of baptism, to show that our sins are forgiven.

The reader places the water on the table with the crown, the scroll and the coins, or at the base of the Advent candle.

The child lights the first, second and third Advent candles.

Prayer for the week

Lord Jesus, help us not only to be prepared to celebrate your coming, but truly to rejoice at the promise of it.

ADVENT 4: A SONG OF PRAISE

LUKE 1:39–55

The fourth reader walks forward, accompanied by a child who carries a 'song of praise'. When they reach the front of the church, the fifth reader joins them from the side.

Fourth reader

I am Mary. I am the Lord's servant and I am to be the mother of the son of God.

Fifth reader

I am Elizabeth. 'Why should the mother of my Lord come to me? God has blessed you more than any other woman! He has also blessed the child you will have. As soon as I heard your greeting, my baby became happy and moved within me. The Lord has blessed you because you believed that he will keep his promise.'
LUKE 1:42–45

The child passes the song of praise to the fourth reader (Mary), who holds it up for all to see and says:

I bring as a symbol a song of praise.

The fourth reader holds up the card with the words of the Magnificat on it and continues:

With all my heart I praise the Lord, and I am glad because of God my Saviour. God cares for me, his humble servant. From now on, all people will say God has blessed me. God All-Powerful has done great things for me, and his name is holy. He always shows mercy to everyone who worships him. The Lord has used his powerful arm to scatter those who

are proud. He drags strong rulers from their thrones and puts humble people in places of power. God gives the hungry good things to eat, and sends the rich away with nothing. He helps his servant Israel and is always merciful to his people. The Lord made this promise to our ancestors, to Abraham and his family for ever!

LUKE 1:46–55

The fourth reader places the card on the table with the crown, scroll, coins and water, or at the base of the Advent candle.

The child lights the four Advent candles.

Prayer for the week

As we read and reflect on this story, may the joy of these two women touch us too.

CHRISTMAS DAY: THE SAVIOUR IS BORN

LUKE 2:10–12, 14

This short introduction to the start of the Christmas Day service could be done with minimum preparation and include any extra children visiting on the day. Choose an older child as the narrator and then ask any children who know they will be at the Christmas service to dress up as angels. Give the children the first and last lines of the script to learn. Any extra children attending on the day could, if they wish, be given a headdress of tinsel to wear.

At the beginning of the service, without introduction, have a group of children walk down the aisle dressed as angels. As they reach the front of the church they turn to the congregation and say together:

Don't be afraid! We have good news for you, which will make everyone happy.

Narrator or older child

This very day in King David's home town a Saviour was born for you. He is Christ the Lord. You will know who he is, because you will find him dressed in baby clothes and lying in a bed of hay.

All children wave hands in the air and say together:

Praise God in heaven! Peace on earth to everyone!

The narrator lights the Advent candles and the service continues with the hymn, 'O come, all ye faithful'.

SHARING LIFE THROUGH ADVENT WITH CHILDREN

INTRODUCTION

The word Advent means 'coming' and is the point in the Christian year when we get ready to celebrate the time when Jesus came to earth as a tiny baby. It is also the time when we look forward to when Jesus will come again. Jesus tells us that when he comes again, the world will be made new. There will be no more fighting and crying, no more pain and sickness.

Sometimes, with all the preparation for Christmas Day—the decorations, parties and presents—we can see Advent just as a kind of countdown to Christmas Day itself instead of a time to get ourselves ready. But how do we get ourselves ready and what does that mean?

This Advent our readings will give us some clues as to how we can use Advent as a time of getting ready to celebrate the mystery of Christmas, and to remind ourselves how God wants us to live now, and until Jesus comes again.

TO MAKE AN ADVENT WREATH

This Advent you might like to make an Advent wreath in the first session with the children, so that you can light it each week of Advent as part of 'Candle time'.

> **You will need:**
> ★ A ring of oasis
> ★ Sprigs of evergreen
> ★ One pink and three purple candles for the outside ring. (Do not light the pink candle until Advent 3)
> ★ One white candle for the centre

Fasten the oasis ring on to a board (a cake board or garden tray would be ideal). Place the four candles at equal distances around the ring. Decorate the rest of the oasis ring with the greenery. Fix a candle holder in the centre of the ring to hold the white candle.

ADVENT 1: SPOTTING THE SIGNS

JEREMIAH 33:14–16; LUKE 21:25–36

SETTING THE SCENE

The word Advent means 'coming' and is the time in the Christian calendar when we get ready to remember how God sent his son Jesus into the world as a tiny baby. Each year at Christmas we celebrate his birthday. But Advent is also the time when we look back to things that have happened in the past and look forward to the time when Jesus said he will come again. You may wish to refer to the introduction on page 76 for further ideas about this.

OPENING ACTIVITY

As children arrive, engage them in putting together the Advent wreath. Details for making the wreath are in the introduction opposite.

WONDERING

Gather the children into a circle and have a variety of Advent calendars, Advent candles, Advent activity books and the Advent wreath for them to look at.

- I wonder which of these you like the best?
- I wonder which is your favourite kind of Advent calendar? (The answer will probably be 'the ones with chocolate'!)
- I wonder what Advent is really about?

Advent means 'coming'—the time when we remember Jesus coming as a baby, and the time when we look forward to Jesus' promise that, one day, he will come again and make all things new. That means an end to things like pain and crying, fighting and cheating!

We can spot the signs of when it is getting close to Christmas because the shops put up their Christmas decorations. But how good are we at spotting signs of other things?

How would you spot the signs for:

- When it's going to rain?
- When it's time to get up?
- When it's autumn?
- When the spring is coming?

How will we know when it is time for Jesus to come again? The answer is that we don't, but we need to be always ready.

PICTURING THE BIBLE

Read Jeremiah 33:14–16 and Luke 21:25–36 and talk about what the writers are saying. You could use some of these reflection pointers to help with the discussion.

- I wonder what this story is about?
- I wonder how this story makes you feel?
- Luke 21:27 says, 'The Son of Man will be seen, coming in a cloud with great power and glory.' I wonder how you might draw this as a picture?

Give the children time to reflect on the story and then read what Jesus said in Luke 21:25: 'Strange things will happen to the sun, moon, and stars.' But Jesus also said that all those who follow him need not be afraid. He says to them, 'When all this starts happening, stand up straight and be brave. You will soon be set free' (Luke 21:28). In other words, there is nothing to be afraid of, for Jesus will be in charge and will be proud of you because you belong to God.

CRAFT ACTIVITY: STAR PICTURE FRAMES

You will need:
Two rectangles of card 15cm x 10cm
Silver sticky stars
Silver foil and yellow gummed paper
Scissors
Polaroid camera (optional)

If a Polaroid camera is available, take individual photographs of the children. However, if instant photographs are not available, encourage the children to take their frame home and find a photograph to put in it.

1. Carefully cut a hole in one of the pieces of card to leave a 3cm frame all the way around. Decorate this frame of card with stars, moons and sun shapes.
2. Sandwich the photograph between the two pieces of card and stick them together.
3. From the leftover piece of card that you cut out of the centre of the picture frame, cut a triangle shape. Fasten this to the back of the card as a stand for the photograph frame.

CANDLE TIME

Play a piece of quiet reflective music as the children gather into a circle. Place the Advent wreath in the centre of the circle. Turn the music down and invite one of the children to light the first candle on the Advent wreath.

Say, 'We look forward to celebrating Jesus' birthday.' *Pause.*

Say, 'We can look forward to Jesus coming again to make everything new.'

Explain that making new is about an end to the pain and suffering of people hurting one another. Ask the children, 'I wonder what you would ask Jesus to make new?'

Pause.

Pass around a little basket containing some silver or coloured stars. Invite the children to take a star and name the thing they would like Jesus to make 'new' in the world. Then invite them to place their star near or on the Advent wreath.

Pause.

Turn the music up. When it has finished, close with the prayer for the week.

PRAYER FOR THE WEEK

Dear Lord Jesus, thank you that you promise that one day you will come again and make everything new. Please help us to take care of your world and to remember those in the world today who are sad and alone and frightened.

ADVENT 2: GETTING OURSELVES READY

MALACHI 3:1–4; LUKE 3:1–6

SETTING THE SCENE

John the Baptist calls the people to turn away from the things they do that will not please God and get ready to meet the Messiah for whom they've been waiting so long. John echoes the words from the prophet Isaiah: 'Get the road ready for the Lord! Make a straight path for him' (Luke 3:4).

OPENING ACTIVITY

As the children arrive, have ready some polishing cloths, water and washing soap, silver and brass polish and some items that need cleaning. These could be the candlesticks, chalice, paten and so on from the church, or items such as dirty cloths or dirty coins.

NB: If children are using chemical cleaning materials, ensure that they wear plastic gloves.

While the children are busy cleaning, remind them that it is the second Sunday of Advent, and that Advent is more than just a countdown to Christmas. Advent is a time to think about getting ourselves ready. When all the cleaning is completed, place it on a table and invite the children to sit in a circle.

WONDERING

Think together about what happens if you are expecting visitors, or a special event like a baby being born, a birthday, a wedding, a baptism or a party. What would you need to do to get ready? Allow time for children to respond. They may suggest things like:

- Clean the house
- Prepare special food
- Buy presents
- Put up decorations

You also have to get yourselves ready. You may have new or special clothes to wear. I wonder what you would do if you knew Jesus was coming to your house?

Explain that today's story took place after Jesus was born and had grown up. A man called John the Baptist began to tell the people that they needed to get themselves ready because Jesus was coming very soon! Look together at Luke 3:3–5. John didn't tell the people to clean their houses, or prepare special food, or put on new clothes. He told the people that they needed to get themselves ready on the inside. He told people it was time to stop doing the things they knew were wrong and to say they were sorry. As a sign that they were willing to change and live as God wanted—and so that they would be ready to welcome Jesus the new king—John invited the people to be baptized right there in the River Jordan.

Ask the children if they have been baptized. What was special about their baptism? Where did it happen? Today at baptisms we give people a candle to show that they have turned from darkness to light. Jesus was often called the light of the world because he showed people how to turn from all that was wrong to what was right.

In the same way, prophets in the Old Testament talked about how the people needed to stop doing the things they knew were wrong, but the prophets used different pictures to explain how God wanted them to be clean on the inside. Sometimes they called this being 'purified' or 'made pure'.

PICTURING THE BIBLE

Read Malachi 3:1–4 and Luke 3:1–6 and talk about what the writers are saying. The images used in this story are the refiner's fire and the launderer's soap. The heat of the refiner's fire was intense in order to separate the dross from the molten pure metal. Similarly, the launderer in those days washed clothes using a strong lye soap, after which the clothes would be placed on a rock and beaten with a stick (see Malachi 3:2b–3a).

- I wonder how you would paint this as a picture?
- I wonder which part of the story you like the best?

When we think about how to get ourselves ready at Advent to celebrate Jesus' birth at Christmas, it's a good opportunity to think about what we are doing and to say 'sorry' for those things we know are wrong.

CRAFT ACTIVITY: LANTERNS IN THE DARK

You will need:
★ Jam jars (one for each child)
★ String
★ Tissue paper in various colours
★ Invisible ink pen or magic marker pen
★ Glue
★ Tealight candles

1. Tie the string securely round the top of the jam jar to make a handle.
2. Tear small pieces of different coloured tissue paper. On some of the pieces of paper, carefully write, with the invisible ink pen, those things that you want to say 'sorry' for.
3. Glue the paper pieces in a mosaic-like pattern all over the outside of the jar. Make sure all the gaps on the jar are filled.
4. Place a tealight candle in the bottom of the jar. You will need to use a long match or taper to light the candle.

NB: Remind the children never to light a candle without an adult being present.

CANDLE TIME

Play a piece of quiet reflective music. Gather the children into a circle. In the centre of the circle place the Advent wreath and around it place the children's lanterns.

Invite a child to light the first and second Advent candle on the Advent wreath. *Pause.*

Invite the children to think about the words they have secretly written on their lanterns. Jesus knows the thought of our hearts and he hears us when we are really sorry. *Pause.*

Jesus loves us and wants to shine the light of his love through us to others.

In turn, light each of the children's lanterns and reaffirm God's love for each of them. Name the children as the lanterns are lit, with the words, '(Name)… Jesus loves you.'

Pause when all the lanterns are lit.

PRAYER FOR THE WEEK

Paul, a follower of Jesus, prayed this beautiful prayer for those who were following Jesus. We can pray it today for each other.

I pray that your love will keep on growing and that you will fully know and understand how to make the right choices. Then you will still be pure and innocent when Christ returns. (Philippians 1:9–10)

If the children are rejoining the adult congregation for Holy Communion or the end of the service, they could return the cleaned articles to their rightful places. If appropriate, this could be carried out as part of the service by involving the children in preparing the table for Holy Communion—for example, placing the candle holders, chalice, paten and so on on the altar.

ADVENT 3: BE JOYFUL

LUKE 3:7–18 AND ZEPHANIAH 3:14–20

SETTING THE SCENE

The third Sunday of Advent is often called 'Gaudete Sunday'. *Gaudeo* is a Latin word meaning 'rejoice'. Traditionally, the third candle on the Advent ring is pink as a symbol of rejoicing as we wait for the coming of Jesus. (Some churches light the pink candle on the fourth Sunday of Advent for the annunciation.)

OPENING ACTIVITY

As children arrive, have a table set ready with biscuits to be iced as 'happy biscuits'. Encourage the children to decorate the biscuits with happy faces or things that make them happy.

> **You will need:**
> ★ Rich tea biscuits
> ★ Ready-made tubes of coloured icing
> ★ Decorations—mini sweets, hundreds and thousands, silver balls

Check the children's health records for allergies or diabetes. When the children have all decorated a biscuit, place the biscuits on one side for later. Ensure there are a few extra biscuits ready decorated for any children who arrive late.

WONDERING

Gather together in a circle. Have a collection of different sized presents wrapped up. (You will need five if you are using the presents to tell this week's story.) In one of the small presents have a packet of sweets or small box of chocolates. Write a gift tag on the present to one of the adult helpers. Talk to the children about giving and receiving presents. Ask the children:

- Who likes presents?
- What would be their favourite Christmas present?
- Do they like giving presents?
- Do they like little presents or big presents?

Pick up the present with the tag on it and read out the name on the tag. Ask the children if they think [name of helper] should be allowed to open the present. When the present is opened, invite the helper to talk to the children about whether she/he should eat all the sweets themselves or share with the children. Of course, they share with the children. Enjoy sharing the gift together.

How would it have felt not to share? Talk about how there are people in our world who are hungry because we don't share the resources of the world fairly. Remember talking last week about how, when Jesus comes again, the world will be made new. Then there will be enough for everyone! In the meantime, we have to think about how we willingly share all that we have.

PICTURING THE BIBLE

Read Luke 3:7–18 and Zephaniah 3:14–20 and talk about what the writers are saying. Remind the children that last week we heard how John the Baptist told the people that the Messiah would be coming soon and that they needed to get themselves ready to meet him.

- I wonder what John is saying to the people?
- I wonder what the people think about John?
- I wonder where you would like to be in the story?
- I wonder what you would like to ask John?

In today's reading, the people continue to come to John to ask him what they need to do to get ready to meet the new king, the promised Messiah. Tell the story from Luke 3:10–15 using the other four wrapped-up gift parcels to tell the story. Have the four presents wrapped up with the following items.

Gift 1: Two lightweight jackets. 'If you have two coats, give one to someone who doesn't have any' (v. 11).
Gift 2: Food, such as a bag of crisps. 'If you have food, share it with someone else' (v. 11).
Gift 3: Chocolate coins. [Tax collectors…] 'Don't make people pay more than they owe' (v. 13).
Gift 4: Chocolate coins. [Soldiers…] 'Don't force people to pay money to make you leave them alone' (v. 14).

On each gift put a gift label with the words of John written on it. As each part of the story is told, invite a child to open the parcel and do whatever the label says.

John told the people to be generous all the time, even to the people they didn't know. He told the people not to cheat others or to take what was not rightfully theirs. At Christmas, we give gifts to those we care about, but Jesus asks us to be generous all the time to those we know as well as to those we don't know.

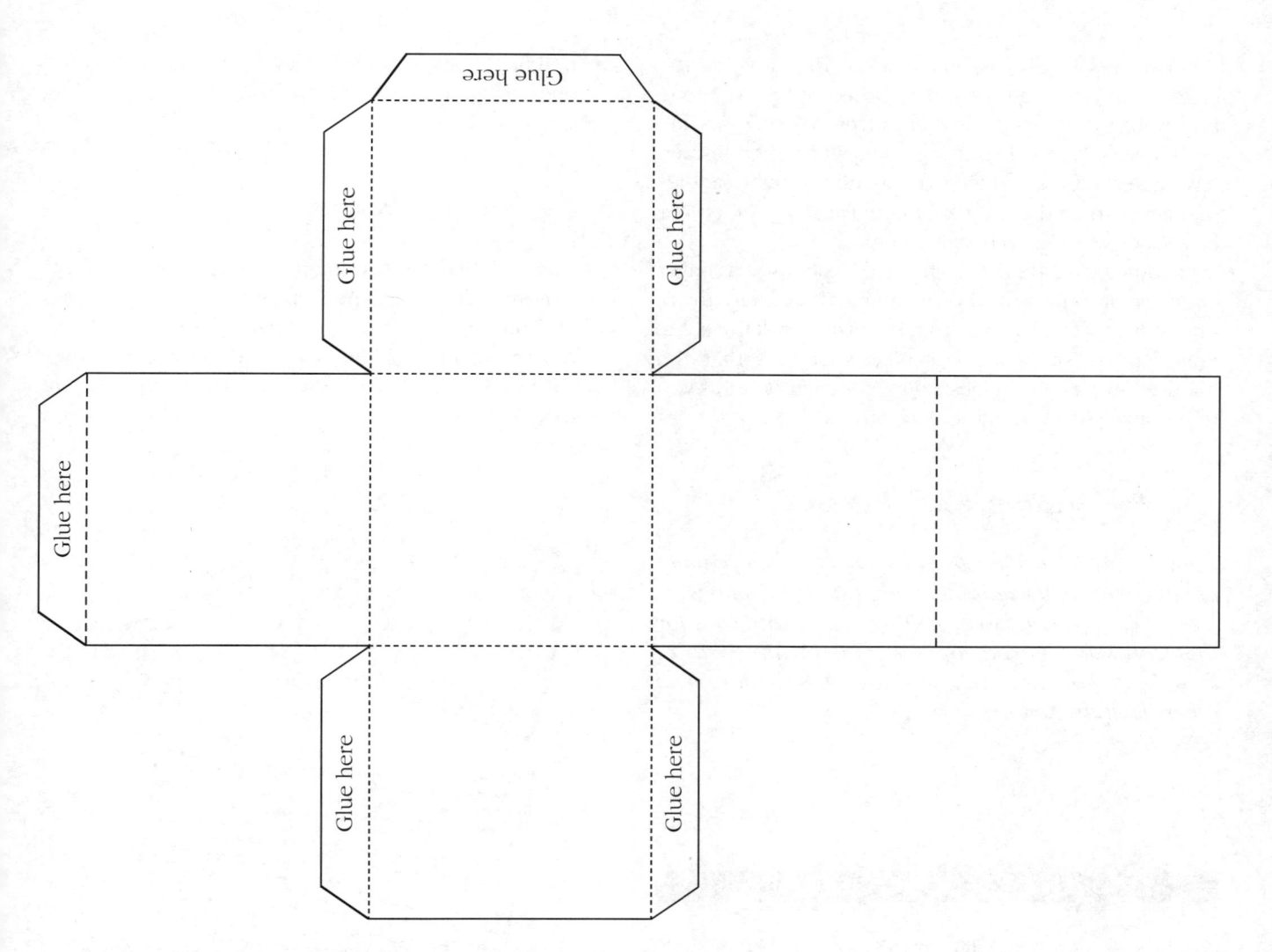

Being generous isn't just about giving gifts, it's about the way we behave towards one another—being kind and thoughtful, looking out for each other—not to make you feel good but because you really care. Jesus wants each of us to be 'joyful givers'.

CRAFT ACTIVITY: A JOYFUL GIVER CUBE

You will need:
- Template of box on thick card
- Thin card, white or coloured
- Glue or double-sided sticky tape
- Felt-tipped pens
- Scissors
- Ruler
- Magazines

1. Draw round the template and carefully cut out the box. Using a ruler and closed scissors, carefully score along fold lines.
2. In three of the box faces/squares, draw or cut out pictures of people who need help. On the other three faces/squares, draw, cut out from magazines or write ways in which you can be a 'joyful giver'.
3. Fold the shape and glue the tabs in place.
4. The cube could have a slot cut in the top, to make it into a money box in which children could be encouraged to collect loose change for a particular group who need help.
5. Alternatively, it could be used as a prayer cube. Roll the cube. If the face on top shows a picture of someone who needs help, pray for that person or those people. If the face on top shows a word or picture about how to be a 'joyful giver', ask God to help you.

CANDLE TIME

Play a piece of quiet reflective music. Gather the children into a circle. In the centre of the circle place the Advent wreath and some of the 'joyful giver' cubes that the children have just made. Point to the pink candle in the wreath and explain to the children that this week in Advent is sometimes called Gaudete Sunday. The word *gaudete* means 'rejoice, be joyful, be happy'.

Share the 'happy biscuits' made earlier, inviting the children to give the biscuit they decorated to someone else rather than eating it themselves. When everyone has a biscuit, enjoy being together. When the children have eaten their biscuits, invite a child to light candles one and two, and the pink candle. Pause to remember how God wants us to be a joyful giver.

If you have made the 'joyful giver' cube into a prayer cube, use it to pray for those who need our help. Invite one or two of the children to take turns to roll the cube. Pray for the situation or similar situations that the picture on the dice suggests. Pray for each other as you think of ways to be generous to others.

PRAYER FOR THE WEEK

Dear heavenly Father, thank you that you promise always to be with us and that you refresh us with your love. Help us always to be willing to help and care for those around us who are sad and in any kind of trouble. Remind us always to share what we have with others joyfully. Amen

✶

ADVENT 4: A SONG OF PRAISE

LUKE 1:39–55

SETTING THE SCENE

The angel Gabriel came to the little town of Nazareth, to the home of a young teenager called Mary, and there he told her the amazing news that God had chosen her to be the mother of the promised Messiah, God's own son. Mary was to call the baby Jesus. The angel also told Mary that her relative Elizabeth, who everyone thought was too old to have a baby, was also pregnant and was going to have a son. The angel said, 'Nothing is impossible with God.' A short time later, Mary hurried off to visit Elizabeth to share her news.

OPENING ACTIVITY

As the children arrive, have a number of seemingly impossible tasks for them to complete, such as:

- Balancing a paper plate on the end of a stick
- Fitting a large object into a small box
- Walking with a balloon balanced on a teaspoon
- Threading beads on to a shoelace
- Building a whole pack of playing cards into a tower, one card at a time, or completing the block building game of 'Jenga'.

WONDERING

Gather the children together into a circle and give them one more task. You will need a nativity-scene Christmas card about postcard size, and a pair of scissors.

Ask the children if they have ever wished that they could step inside the nativity scene. Tell them they can! It sounds impossible, but ask them, 'Who believes you can do it?'

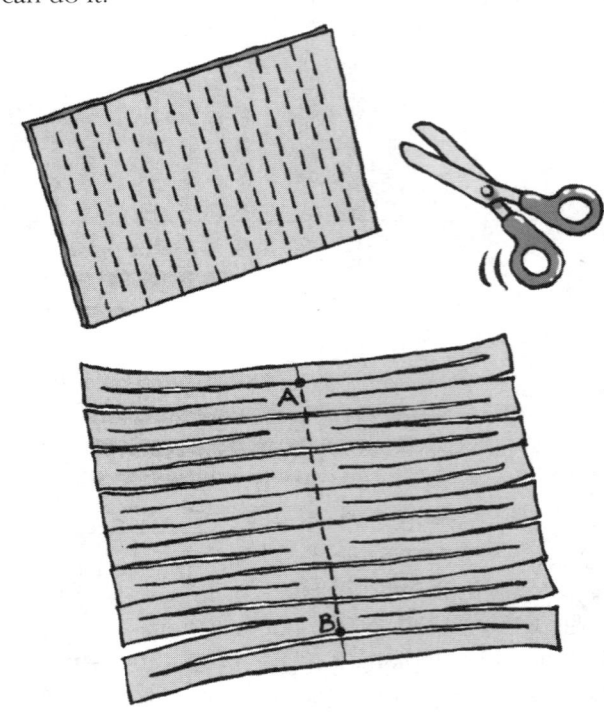

Fold the card in half and make eight cuts along the folded edge, down to about 1 cm from the other edge. Now turn the card round and make seven similar cuts along the open side of the card between the first set of cuts. Open the postcard and make one last cut between points A and B. Now gently open up the cuts and invite a volunteer to 'step inside' the picture. Talk about what it would have been like to really be there.

Ask the children:

- Have you ever been asked to do something that seemed impossible? Was it really impossible or could you do it? How did you feel?
- Have you ever been asked to do something really important? How did that feel?

Remind the children how the angel came to Mary and told her she was going to have a special baby. Mary must have thought that what the angel told her was impossible, but she knew she could trust God and so she said to the angel, 'Let it happen as you have said.' Mary then set off to visit Elizabeth. The angel had told Mary that her relative Elizabeth was also expecting a baby, even though everyone thought she was too old. Elizabeth was to call her baby John, and, as we saw last week, John had a very important part to play in God's plan.

PICTURING THE BIBLE

Read Luke 1:39–55 and talk about the story. Ask the children:

- I wonder which part of the story you like the best?

Mary and Elizabeth must have had so many questions to ask each other when they met, but the first thing they did was to thank and praise God. Read Luke 1:41–42 and then verses 46–55. Mary sang a song of praise. This song is often called the Magnificat and, through the centuries, Christians have said or sung it in worship. In her song, Mary praises God for all that he has done in the past and for keeping his promises to his people. She wonders at how God turns things upside-down—valuing those who are often ignored, caring for those who have nothing, and making 'somebodies' out of 'nobodies'.

But Mary wasn't the only one to sing a song of praise to God. On the night that Jesus was born the angels sang songs of praise: 'Praise God in heaven! Peace on earth to everyone who pleases God' (Luke 2:14).

When the shepherds returned from visiting the stable, they also sang songs of praise (Luke 2:20).

CRAFT ACTIVITY

Praise bells (for younger children)

You will need:
- Small plastic plant pot or paper cup
- Silver foil
- Piece of dowel for handle
- Narrow strips of crepe paper in various colours, about 1.5cm wide x 18cm long
- Cat bells (these can be purchased inexpensively from pet or craft shops)
- String
- Double-sided sticky tape
- Strong tape

1. Carefully make a hole in the top of the pot and push the piece of dowel through to make a handle (it might be better for an adult to do this). Secure the handle on the inside with strong tape.
2. Cover the pot in silver foil.
3. Thread two or three cat bells on to a length of string. Fasten string to the top of the pot on the inside.
4. Cut a length of double-sided tape and remove one side of its protective cover. Attach lengths of crepe paper streamers along the length of the tape.
5. Remove second protective cover of the tape and fasten to bottom rim of pot on the inside.

Praise bracelets (for older children)

You will need:
- Beads of various sizes, shapes and colours. (You could cut up old necklaces from charity shops)
- Strong nylon thread or fishing line
- Scissors

Think of five or six things you would like to praise God for. Choose five or six special beads, one for each item of praise. Thread some smaller beads on to the thread and then add a special bead. Continue in this way until the thread is the right length to slip over your wrist. Tie the ends of thread together and trim. Use your bracelet to remind you to praise God at all times and in all places.

CANDLE TIME

Play a piece of joyful music (it could be a Christmas carol). Gather the children into a circle and in the centre of the circle place the Advent wreath.

Have ready four symbols that represent the activities of the four weeks:

Week 1: Stars
Week 2: Lantern and candle
Week 3: Small wrapped gift
Week 4: Bells

Invite four children to hold one of the symbols each. Invite four more children to light the Advent candles.

Leader: We remember that Advent is the time when we look forward to celebrating the birth of Jesus.

Invite the first child to light the first Advent candle.

Leader: Jesus promised that one day he will come again and make everything new.

Invite second child to scatter stars around candle.

All: We will watch for his coming

Younger children ring their praise bells.

Leader: We remember that John told the people to get ready to meet Jesus.

Invite third child to light the Advent candle.

Leader: Jesus came to be the light of the world.

Invite fourth child to place the lantern by the Advent wreath.

All: We will shine as light for him.

Younger children ring their praise bells.

Leader: We remember that the pink candle reminds us to rejoice and be happy.

Invite fifth child to light the pink Advent candle.

Leader: Jesus teaches us to be generous at all times.

Invite sixth child to place gift by the Advent wreath.

All: We will be joyful givers.

Younger children ring their praise bells.

Leader: We remember that Mary sang a song of praise when she heard God's promise that she was to be the mother of Jesus.

Invite seventh child to light the fourth Advent candle.

Leader: The angels and the shepherds sang songs of praise when the baby was born.

Invite eighth child to lay bells by the Advent wreath.

All: We too will sing songs of praise.

Younger children ring their praise bells.

Finish the session by singing together one of the children's favourite carols, accompanied by the praise bells.

SHARING LIFE THROUGH ADVENT WITH FAMILIES

INTRODUCTION

Christmas can be a season fraught with activity and busyness. We can often arrive at Christmas Day having forgotten what the real celebration is about. Here are some ideas for how the whole family can make the important countdown to Christmas more meaningful and exciting. At the heart of all celebrations there is a place for:

- Story
- Symbol
- Sharing
- Remembering and often resolution

In each of the four weeks of Advent, you will see these four themes recurring. You will be encouraged to discover the significance of colour, create your own family prayers, share stories, decorate the home, prepare special foods and maybe even have time to play a game or two.

Some families may set aside a time each day to light the candle and share the ideas, maybe during a shared meal. Other families may find it easier to set aside time just once a week. Either way, with the use of the four Bible passages, candle and suggestions for different family activities, you can do as little or as much as you choose, or as time allows.

So join in the Advent journey and follow us all the way to Bethlehem!

KEY TO ACTIVITIES

Light the candle

Thinking about the story

Themes to explore

Pray together

Things to make

Games to play

IDEAS FOR USING THE MATERIAL

- As a family, decide whether you are going to light the candle at the meal table, or whether you are going to set up a special focus space where the candle might be placed. This might be on a special table or shelf.
- Decide when you might share this special time together. It might be at a mealtime, at bedtime or even during the weekend.
- Use a modern version of the Bible for the readings.
- Involve different members of the family in reading the Bible passage.
- Don't be afraid to repeat the reading of the same passage over several days. Different things might come out of the passage with repeated reading.
- Encourage each member of the family to contribute to any conversation about the passage or the picture if they wish to, and really listen to each other.
- In some churches, the Christian festivals are marked by special liturgical colours. This might be picked up in the clothes worn by the minister or on altar frontals or cloths. The liturgical colour for Advent is purple. As a family, you might want to mark this special time by using a purple cloth or serviettes at the table. They might be paper cloths and serviettes, or the children might like to make special place-mats decorated in purple.
- Follow the instructions and make a Christmas garland to hang on your Christmas tree or in your house. Each week there will be ideas for adding a different symbol to your garland. The finished garland will tell the story of your journey through Advent.
- Where young children are involved, take special care with the lighting and positioning of the candle. Do not leave matches where children can reach them.

YEAR C

ADVENT 1

SPOTTING THE SIGNS

JEREMIAH 33:14–16; LUKE 21:25–36

Light the candle and read Jeremiah 33:14–16. The word Advent means 'coming' and today's reading reminds us that Advent is the time when we remember God's promise to his people that one day a king would come from the family of David—a king who, unlike many others, would be honest and would rule fairly. Christians believe that God is talking about his own son, Jesus. Advent is the time when we remember Jesus coming as a baby into the world. If, however, we look at the second of this week's readings, we will see that it points towards yet another coming.

Look together at Luke 21:25–28. Here Jesus point us to the time when he will come again.

- I wonder what shapes you can see in the stars at night?
- I wonder if you have ever seen a shooting star?
- I wonder if you have ever seen an eclipse of the sun? What do you remember about it?

If using the material daily, you could explore a different theme on different days.

- **Coming**: Today's readings talk about the coming of two very special events. Talk together about how you prepare for special events. Is there anything that you are particularly looking forward to as you prepare for this Christmas?
- **Christmas**: This is a special time in the year to look forward to. What are some of your family traditions associated with Christmas? Make a list together of all that has to be done in the weeks running up to Christmas. Who will be responsible for doing which of the jobs? Is there something you can do that will remind you as a family what Christmas is really about? You may talk about how you will use this family material in the coming weeks.
- **Spotting the signs**: Talk together about different things that people go spotting—for example bird spotting, train or plane spotting. Advent is a time when we remember how Jesus told the people (in Luke 21:29–33) to watch out for the signs of when he would come again. Talk together about how this reading makes you feel. Is it scary, exciting or something else?
- **Looking to the stars**: It's not unusual for people to look at the stars for signs; people throughout the centuries have been doing this. Look together at Matthew 2:1–2. Here we see that the wise men from the east had been looking to the stars for the birth of a new king. When they saw a new star, they left their homes and followed it all the way to Bethlehem. You might like to look together in a book or on a computer at the different shapes that the stars make in the sky. See how the different star shapes have different names. When it's dark, you could go outside and see what stars you can see in the night sky.
- **Making things new**: The reading in Jeremiah pointed to the coming of a new and special king who would rule with honesty and justice. Jesus was that king, and yet he still pointed forward to a time when he would return and put an end to all fighting and hatred, pain and sadness. I wonder what you would change about the world?

Sharing life through Advent with families

For the prayer time, you will need a picture or map of the world and some silver stars.

You might be particularly attentive to the news this week, either on children's television, the radio or in newspapers. Think together about what the world is like. What are some of the things that are happening in the world that you would like to see changed? As you identify a situation you would like to change, place a star on the map and ask for God's love to reach that place.

Pray for today's leaders, that they may rule honestly and fairly just as Jesus taught us.

THE BRIGHTEST STAR

Make a star decoration for your door to welcome visitors into your home this Christmas.

You will need:
* Three sheets of shiny wrapping paper in contrasting colours
* Christmas bells or some Christmas ribbon
* Double-sided sticky tape
* Thin card
* Stapler and scissors

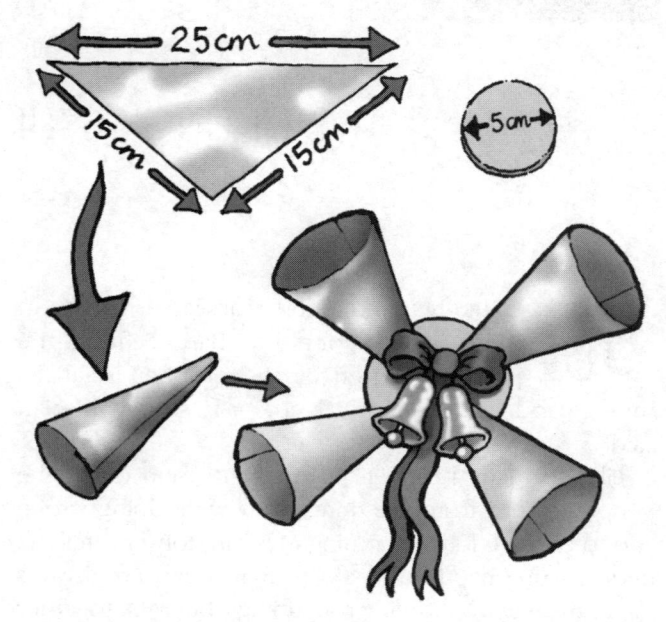

1. Cut out four triangles of each colour, approximately 25cm x 15cm x 15cm. Roll each triangle into a cone shape and fasten the two edges with double-sided sticky tape.
2. Cut a circle out of the card, approximately 5cm in diameter.
3. Place all twelve cones on to the card with their points facing the centre. Keeping the ends of the cones open, staple each cone to the card.
4. Attach the bells or curled Christmas ribbon to the centre.

YEAR C

ADVENT 2

GETTING OURSELVES READY

MALACHI 3:1–4; LUKE 3:1–6

Light the candle and read Luke 3:2b–6. In these verses, John the Baptist fulfils the promise written by the prophet Isaiah all those years ago. Look at Isaiah 40:3–5 to see what Isaiah said.

Like so many prophets before him, John called the people to turn from the things they were doing wrong and to prepare for the coming Messiah. John invites the people to be baptized as a sign that they were serious about turning from their wrongdoings, but look together at the very last book of the Old Testament to see what image the prophet Malachi uses to tell the people how they need to change their ways (Malachi 3:1–4).

Think about the story together and talk about what the writers are saying.

- I wonder what image you would use to show what it means to be purified?

If using the material daily, you could explore a different theme on different days.

- **A rallying call**: Remember together if you have ever been somewhere—maybe to a procession or a parade—where the leader makes a call for everyone to be ready. The band becomes poised to play and the parade gets ready to move off. I wonder how you felt or how you think you might feel? I wonder how the people felt when they heard Isaiah, and later John, telling them to get ready?
- **A promise fulfilled**: Talk together about promises. Have you ever made a promise? How do you feel waiting for a promise to come true? Has anyone ever broken a promise to you? How did that make you feel? The prophet Isaiah told the people that God promised to send a messenger to announce that the Messiah was coming. This week's reading shows how God kept his promise. What other promises did God make? What does God promise us today?
- **Special messages**: Advent is the time when we send special messages of love to people—often to people that we don't see very often. I wonder if you have received any Christmas cards yet? Look at the cards together and remember the people who have sent them. Talk together about people to whom you will be sending Christmas cards this year. You might even write a family letter together to send with the cards.

- **Who was John?**: Look together at Luke 1:5–24 and Luke 1:39–45. The Bible doesn't tell us much about what happened to John and Jesus as they grew up, but clearly John had an important job to do for God in preparing people for Jesus' coming. Some people even asked John if he was the Messiah. Look at Luke 3:15–16 to see what John replied.
- **Getting ourselves ready**: John baptized the people in the River Jordan as a sign that they were going to turn from the things that they were doing wrong. If any member of the family has been baptized, talk about what happened at their baptism. Look at any photographs that might have been taken. Talk about how we need to go on doing what is right and how we need to say 'sorry' when we get things wrong.

Hold a teaspoon and think about the letters 'tsp'. When we pray, we can say **t**hank you to God for all that he has promised, **s**orry for the things that we get wrong and **p**lease for anything that we want to ask God for. The abbreviated letters for teaspoon can remind us of these three prayers.

Pass the teaspoon round the table, allowing each member of the family to pray—starting with a thank you prayer, then a sorry prayer, a please prayer, then back to a thank you prayer again and so on around the table.

Sharing life through Advent with families

CHRISTMAS MESSAGES

Send your own special Christmas messages in these simple Christmas cards.

You will need:
* Pieces of paper or thin card in different colours, approximately 21 cm x 15 cm (A5)
* Scissors and glue
* Felt-tipped pens
* Glitter

1. Fold in the two short edges of the paper to meet in the centre.
2. Carefully draw a curved line on the top edge of the paper and cut along it so that the shape looks like two closed doors. Colour the front folded pieces brown to look like the stable doors.
3. Open the flaps and you will have three panels. In the centre panel draw Mary and Joseph and the baby Jesus. In one side panel draw the shepherds visiting, or the donkey. In the second side panel draw the angel.
4. Carefully dab some glue along the inside curved edges of the picture and sprinkle with glitter. Now turn your card over and write your special Christmas message on the back.

YEAR C

ADVENT 3

BE JOYFUL

ZEPHANIAH 3:14–20; LUKE 3:7–18

Light the candle and read Luke 3:7–18. John warns the people that it is no good coming to be baptized unless they truly intend to change their actions. He even warns the Jews that they cannot rely on their family history to save them. True repentance, he warns, is only born out of action. Then, in response to the crowd's questions, John gives some specific examples of how their behaviour must change.

Think about the story together and talk about what the writer is saying.

- I wonder if any children were among the crowds that went to see John?
- I wonder what the people thought of John?
- I wonder where you would put yourself in the story as part of the crowd?

If using the material daily, you could explore a different theme on different days.

- **Shopping lists**: Give each member of the family a piece of paper. On the top of the paper write, 'If I had a million pounds I would buy … (name of person) a … (present).' Invite each member of the family to write or draw a shopping list of the presents they would buy for each member of the family. When everyone has completed the lists, share your imaginary gift lists with each other.
- **Gifts of the heart**: Give each member of the family another piece of paper. This time, on the top of the paper write, 'If I had no money I would give … (name of person) a … (present).' As before, share the imaginary gift lists with each other. Think about the two lists of presents. I wonder which gifts are the most special?
- **Being a joyful giver**: Talk about what it feels like to give gifts, and what it's like receiving gifts. As we have seen, some gifts don't have to cost anything. They are about how we treat one another. John told the people not to be reluctant in the way they treated people but to give generously to everyone.
- **Share a gift**: Think together about the people who won't enjoy a warm house, good food, friends and Christmas presents this Christmas. Think about the people who live on the streets in this country, young people who have run away from home, and children in other parts of the world who never know Christmas. Find out if there is someone in your area collecting gifts for children in homes or overseas. Together make up a gift to send.
- **Enough for all to share**: Jesus promised that one day he will come again, and on that day he will make all things new. Think together what it would be like to live in a world where there is no more pain and sorrow, no more hunger and disease. Talk about what you can do as a family to help today. It might be to buy Fair Trade goods in the supermarket, or give money and clothes to charities. It may be to find out more about a particular project and to pray for that situation.

Have a collection of gift tags available, enough for each member of the family. Invite each member to draw or write a short prayer on the gift tag, highlighting one of the areas that you have talked about as a family. It might be about giving gifts to one another or to those less fortunate. It might be to pray for those who are lonely and without a family to share Christmas with, or it might be for those in the world who are hungry and lonely.

When the prayers are all written, hang the tags on different door handles around the house. This way, you can remember to pray for that situation whenever you go through the door.

Sharing life through Advent with families

YEAR C

GIFTS FROM THE HEART

You will need:
- Stiff card
- Thin card
- Small pieces of wrapping paper
- Coloured tissue paper
- Small pieces of paper
- Sugared almonds or Christmas tree chocolate
- Heart-shaped confetti
- Christmas ribbon
- Scissors
- Glue

5. Place two or three sugared almonds or chocolates in the tissue paper and place them in the heart with a sprinkling of heart-shaped confetti.
6. Write on the piece of paper who the gift is for and who it is from, and glue the paper on the front of the heart shape. Hang the heart shapes on the Christmas tree.

1. Draw a heart-shape template on stiff card and cut it out.
2. Glue one piece of thin card to a piece of wrapping paper. Draw round the template to give two heart shapes on the card. Cut the two shapes out.
3. Carefully glue the straight edges of the heart together, leaving the top open like a pocket.
4. Make a hole in the middle at the top of the heart. Thread some Christmas ribbon through the two holes and fasten.

Sharing life through Advent with families

Reproduced with permission from *Sharing Life through Advent* published by BRF 2004 (1 84101 306 4)

YEAR C

ADVENT 4

A SONG OF PRAISE

LUKE 1:39–55

Light the candle and read Luke 1:39–55. The angel has visited Mary and told her that she is to be the mother of God's son, and she is to call him Jesus. Mary goes off to the nearby village to see her relative Elizabeth and to tell her the good news. The angel has told Mary that Elizabeth is also having a baby. Mary and Elizabeth are so happy to see each other and to know that God has been true to his word. Mary sings a song of praise and thanks to God, a song that we still sing today in the words of the Magnificat.

Think about the story together and talk about what the writer is saying.

- I wonder which part of the story you like the best?
- I wonder what Mary is really thinking?
- I wonder what Elizabeth is thinking as she greets Mary?

If using the material daily, you could explore a different theme on different days.

- **A baby boy**: Today, many mothers can find out if their baby is going to be a boy or a girl, even before the baby is born, by having a special test called a scan. For Mary, it was the angel who told her that her baby was going to be a boy and that his name would be Jesus. Talk about other names you might have been given when you were born, and if your parents knew whether you were going to be a boy or a girl.
- **A happy meeting**: Something special had happened to both Mary and Elizabeth, so it wasn't surprising that they were very excited when they met. They recognized that this was God at work in their lives and they remembered to thank him. Talk together about any time when you feel God did something special in your life. It might be something quite small, but special all the same.
- **Mary the mother of Jesus**: God had chosen Mary to be the mother of Jesus. Mary said, 'From now on, all people will say God has blessed me' (Luke 1:48). Artists and sculptors across the ages have drawn, painted and made statues of Mary. Look at your Christmas cards and see how many of them have a picture of Mary on them. Think together if your church has a statue, a stained-glass window or a picture of Mary anywhere in it. If not, see if you can find and visit a church that has one.
- **Saying 'thank you'**: Think together about how many different ways there are of saying 'thank you'. We say 'thank you' when we receive gifts at Christmas and we say 'thank you' when someone does something for us, but do we remember to say 'thank you' to God for all that he gives us and does for us?
- **A song of praise**: Look at Mary's song of praise (Luke 1:46–55) and make a list of all that she thanked God for. Now together make a list of all that you would like to thank God for.

Compile a list of thank you prayers as a basis for this prayer activity.

> **You will need:**
> ★ A glass bowl
> ★ Glass nuggets
> ★ Floating candles and matches

Fill the glass bowl with some water and have at the table some glass nuggets and floating candles. Using the list of things you would like to say 'thank you' to God for, take it in turns to place a glass nugget in the water and name one of the items on the list. When all the items have been named, float one or two candles on the water and light them.

Sharing life through Advent with families

Reproduced with permission from *Sharing Life through Advent* published by BRF 2004 (1 84101 306 4)

Quietly think about all that God has given you and say 'thank you' to him. The bowl and floating candles could act as a table decoration for the next few days up to Christmas, as a reminder in the busyness to say 'thank you' to God for all that he has done for you as a family.

CHRISTMAS BAUBLES

Thank God for the gift of each other with these special Christmas baubles.

You will need:
- One plain plastic or fabric bauble for each member of the family
- Runny glue and a paintbrush
- Glitter
- Sheet of paper to catch and recycle the glitter

Using the glue, write the name of a family member on the bauble. Hold the bauble carefully over a sheet of paper and sprinkle glitter over the glue. Leave to dry and then hang on the Christmas tree.

If any member of the family has died this year, you might like to make a bauble to remember them this Christmas.

SHARING LIFE THROUGH ADVENT BIBLE READING NOTES

YEAR C

ADVENT 1

SPOTTING THE SIGNS

JEREMIAH 33:14–16; LUKE 21:25–36

KEY VERSE

So, when you see these things happening, you know that God's kingdom will soon be here.
LUKE 21:31

This passage comes towards the end of a long collection of sayings of Jesus about the 'future'. It stemmed from something he said about the great temple in Jerusalem, that one day it would all be knocked down. Some of his hearers asked when this would happen, and that introduces the theme of the future—especially what some people like to call the 'end times'. In fact, clearly, some of what he was speaking about would be fulfilled quite soon ('some of the people of this generation will still be alive...' v. 32), and most scholars think those sections refer to the destruction of Jerusalem by the Romans in AD70. But other events, culminating in the appearing of the Son of Man 'coming in a cloud with great power and glory' (v. 27) have obviously not happened yet.

What Jesus invites his hearers to do is to be alert to the signs of the times. They were mostly rural people and they knew that seasonal changes were marked by such things as the fig tree putting out its leaves. In the same way, Jesus suggests, we should keep an eye on the spiritual 'signs of the times', so that God's great moments don't catch us by surprise.

However, when Jesus spoke of the Day of the Lord, or even the day of judgment, it was not in order to frighten people, but to give them hope. 'This is still God's world,' he was saying, in effect. 'He's still in charge, however black things may seem. He has a loving purpose—the coming of his kingdom—and that can't be thwarted.'

Jeremiah had a similar message in his day, in today's Old Testament reading. Writing from prison, he had words of hope, looking on to the day when Jerusalem and Judah would live in peace and security. Instead of wallowing in the current situation, he wanted people to renew their trust in God (Jeremiah 33:14–16).

TO THINK ABOUT

When some people are 'so frightened that they will faint' at the sight of the Son of Man coming in glory, Jesus wants his followers to 'stand up straight and be brave'. This is not a fearful event, but the moment when they will 'soon be free' (see Luke 21:26–28). That is why our Advent hymns on this theme often tell us, 'Rejoice, rejoice!'

A PRAYER

You teach us, Lord Jesus, to look for the signs of the coming of your kingdom. Teach us also how to pray for its dawning.

Sharing life through Advent Bible reading notes

YEAR C

ADVENT 2

GETTING OURSELVES READY

MALACHI 3:1–4; LUKE 3:1–6

KEY VERSE

The messenger you desire is coming with my promise, and he is on his way.
MALACHI 3:1

TO THINK ABOUT

Are we ready for his coming? Christmas is like a rehearsal! People weren't ready the first time Jesus came, and mostly failed to recognize him. To prepare our hearts to welcome the child born at Bethlehem 2000 years ago is a good way to prepare ourselves for his next coming 'in glorious majesty'.

A PRAYER

Search our hearts, gracious God, and show us if there is anything impure or harmful there, so that we may turn back to you, know your forgiveness and be ready to welcome you when you come.

The prophet Malachi was speaking to a generation who wondered when, if ever, God was going to come to their rescue. The people of Israel had looked and longed for their 'Messiah'—the one who would lead them into a golden future—for many years. They knew that a 'messenger' would precede him and now they are told that the messenger is on his way.

Well, to be honest, the messenger would be a long while coming, in terms of human time—several hundred years. But come he did, though when he arrived he may not have been quite what they were expecting. Luke sets the scene. The emperor Tiberius and his governor Pilate, assisted by his henchmen Herod, Philip and Lysanias, were the secular rulers. Annas and Caiaphas were the Jewish high priests. In other words, the people of God's covenant were suffering under the absolute rule of the occupying power and the religious rule of a corrupt temple.

In this situation, to whom did God's word come? To John, the son of Zechariah, who was living in the desert, feeding (Mark tells us) on 'grasshoppers and wild honey' and dressed in a camel-hair coat. Could this really be the promised messenger of God, the one they had longed for?

Yet his message fitted the prophecy. Malachi had spoken of the need for the people to be purified, made clean and ready for the coming of the Lord. When the Lord himself came, that cleansing process would be like the fire in the refiner's furnace, where silver is purified. John called the people to get themselves ready to turn back to God and be baptized. Then their sins would be forgiven. They would be ready for the Lord when he came.

Sharing life through Advent Bible reading notes

YEAR C

ADVENT 3

BE JOYFUL

ZEPHANIAH 3:14–20; LUKE 3:7–18

KEY VERSE

Everyone in Jerusalem and Judah, celebrate and shout with all your heart!
ZEPHANIAH 3:14

TO THINK ABOUT

'The Lord your God… is always with you… and he will refresh your life with his love' (Zephaniah 3:17). Think of Christmas as a time when the Lord will 'refresh your life', most of all simply by promising to be with you always.

A PRAYER

Lord Jesus, help us not only to be prepared to celebrate your coming, but truly to rejoice at the promise of it.

This is traditionally known as 'Gaudete Sunday'—a day of rejoicing—probably because of this verse in Zephaniah and also the idea in the Gospel reading that everyone became excited at John's preaching, and were 'filled with expectation' (NRSV). Sometimes we are happy because a really good thing has happened, and sometimes because we *expect* something good to happen.

No one could accuse John of trying to court popularity! It's almost as though he carefully chose each group of people among his hearers to criticize—even those who came running to him for baptism were 'snakes' running away from judgment. Tax collectors, soldiers and even the king, Herod, came under his lash. God was threshing his harvest, separating the wheat from the chaff, and everyone, without exception, must undergo this process of purification.

Despite this, the people flocked to hear him. At last, something was happening, someone was telling them the truth, even if they found it a bit hard to swallow. Finally, Herod had had enough and arrested John and put him in prison.

All that did, of course, was to take the messenger off the stage and put the Messiah, Jesus, on it. The very next chapter of Luke's Gospel tells how Jesus burst on the scene, fresh himself from baptism at the hands of John. The story was now in motion.

Many of us, not just the children, are excited at the prospect of Christmas coming near. There will be friends and relatives to see, parties to enjoy, presents to share. Of course, it can be a painful time, too, when we are very aware of people who *aren't* there any longer, and it's also possible to turn what should be a relaxed and happy time into a stressful one. But obviously it's right to be joyful as we look forward to celebrating the birth of Jesus—by far the most important birthday there has ever been—and to be excited by it!

Sharing life through Advent Bible reading notes

YEAR C

ADVENT 4

A SONG OF PRAISE

LUKE 1:39–55

KEY VERSE

The Lord has blessed you because you believed he will keep his promise.
LUKE 1:45

TO THINK ABOUT

Both Mary and Elizabeth were blessed by God because they believed that he would keep his promise—impossible as it seemed in both cases.

A PRAYER

As we read and reflect on this story, may the joy of these two women touch us, too.

Luke is a gifted writer and this lovely little story of the meeting of Mary and Elizabeth is typical of his skill. It is also typical in that this, in a Gospel full of stories of kindness and humanity, is the first of them. Mary, as we have already noted, was probably no more than a young teenager; Elizabeth, we have already learnt, was 'advanced in years' and childless. Luke tells us that they were related in some way, although they lived far apart—Mary in Nazareth, in Galilee, and Elizabeth in 'the hill country of Judea' around Jerusalem. But Mary, full of her news, can't wait to tell Elizabeth about her pregnancy. No quick phone call or e-mail in those days! So she presumably walked the sixty-odd miles to pay her visit to the older woman, whom the angel had told Mary was now six months pregnant.

What a meeting it turned out to be, as the young girl arrived at the house! As Mary greeted her, Luke says, Elizabeth's baby 'moved within her'. Actually the Greek word is a bit less prosaic—it's usually used for a dance of joy, or the gambolling of lambs, as though the tiny John in the womb wanted to join in the celebration! In the same way, the translation 'became happy' seems rather tepid: the word indicates thrill or delight. This was a wonderful moment and Luke captures it for us—the joy of two expectant mothers and the fulfilment of knowing that in both cases it was possible only through the work of the Holy Spirit.

Elizabeth, the older woman, wife of a priest and herself a member of the priestly line of Aaron, nevertheless greets the youthful Mary with deference as 'the mother of my Lord' and invokes a formal blessing on her: 'God has blessed you more than any other woman! He has also blessed the child you will have.' This, of course, has now become part of the 'Ave Maria' prayer: 'Blessed are you among women and blessed is the fruit of your womb, Jesus.'

Sharing life through Advent Bible reading notes

SHARING LIFE THROUGH COLLECTIVE WORSHIP

ADVENT 1: SPOTTING THE SIGNS

JEREMIAH 33:14–16; LUKE 21:25–36

INTRODUCTION

This first assembly introduces the season of Advent and looks at how the Bible tells us we will be able to recognize the signs of Jesus' coming.

FOCUS

> **You will need:**
> ★ Small table
> ★ Purple cloth to cover the table
> ★ Advent wreath as per p. 80 (without candles)
> ★ Five candles: four purple and one white
> ★ Star shapes cut from silver card
> ★ Seven children to hold the different objects

Welcome the children and then place a small empty table in the front of where they are sitting. Make reference to the empty table and suggest that today is the beginning of a special season in the Christian calendar. Invite the children to watch carefully for clues as to what season it is.

Ask the children holding the objects to bring in the objects carefully one at a time to place on the table as follows:

- The first child places the purple cloth on the table. Explain that purple is the colour for getting ready.
- The second child brings the Advent wreath without any candles and places it in the centre of the table.
- Four children bring the four purple Advent candles. Place the four candles into the holders in the wreath, slowly counting '1, 2, 3, 4'—the four weeks of getting ready.
- The seventh child brings the white candle for the centre of the Advent wreath. Ask the children if they know what the white candle is for. Place the candle in the centre of the wreath. The white candle represents the mystery of Christmas Day, the day when Jesus was born.

Stand back and pause. Ask the children if they know what the time of getting ready for Christmas is called. It's Advent. Explain that these are some of the signs that point to the time when we remember Jesus coming as a tiny baby into the world. Ask the children what signs tell them that:

- Spring is coming.
- It's dinner time.
- It's somebody's birthday.

Advent is the time when we remember that God promised to send a special king who would rule the people with honesty and fairness. Read Jeremiah 33:14–16. Jesus was the new king whom the prophet Jeremiah was talking about.

We know that Jesus was born as a tiny baby in Bethlehem. But, like all babies, he grew up; and when he was a grown up he began to tell the people how much God loved them. He talked about God being their heavenly father, and some people thought this was all a bit strange. Jesus also taught people the ways to be honest and fair and to care for everyone equally, but some people didn't like the things Jesus said and they plotted to have him arrested and put to death.

Before Jesus died, he promised that one day he would come again. He told the people to watch for the signs of his coming.

Jesus told the people to watch the sun, the moon and the stars for signs of his coming. He promised that when he came again he would make all things new. There would be no more fighting and wars, no more crying and pain, no more lying and cheating.

REFLECTION

Light the first Advent candle and play a quiet piece of music. Invite the children to think about a world with no more fighting and cheating, no more pain and sickness, where everything is made new. After a few moments, ask the children to comment on what things they would like Jesus to change and make new in the world. Change these thoughts into prayers.

PRAYER

Have sections of the following prayer written on four star shapes for four children to read. After the act of worship, the star shapes could be threaded together to make a mobile as a reminder of this week's signs of Jesus' coming. (You will find a star template on page 29.)

Star One

Dear Lord Jesus, thank you that you came to earth as a tiny baby and grew up to teach us how to care for one another.

Star Two

Help us to make a difference in our world today, by caring for those who are sad, hurt or lonely.

Star Three

Help us to make things new today by being kind instead of unkind, by sharing what we have with others…

Star Four

… and by loving one another as Jesus taught us. Amen

SONGS

Who made the twinkling stars?
There are hundreds of sparrows

FOLLOW-ON WORK

Talk about star shapes in the night sky and their names. Talk about eclipses of the sun or moon. Spot the signs of winter, and put together a winter table display.

✱

ADVENT 2: GETTING OURSELVES READY

MALACHI 3:1–4; LUKE 3:1–6

INTRODUCTION

This assembly will look at how John the Baptist told the people to get themselves ready to meet Jesus.

FOCUS

As the children arrive, continue to get the room ready with exaggerated movements. Ask a couple of children to sweep the floor. Struggle to put up the screen and projector. Look for the focus table and place it at the front. Give the impression of rushing to get everything ready. Sit down looking exhausted and then remember that the focus table hasn't been set.

Talk the children through the items on the focus table as you set it.

- The purple cloth—the colour in the Christian year for getting ready.
- The Advent wreath with its four purple candles for the four weeks of Advent.
- The white candle for Christmas Day.
- A star to remind us that Jesus told us to watch for the signs of his coming.

Pause and relax. Now that everything is ready, we can begin!

Talk to the children about getting ready. It might be getting ready for a special event or an outing, a birthday party or visitors coming to stay. Talk about how sometimes you have to rush to get everything ready. Talk about the different things that might need to be done.

The people of Israel had been waiting a long time for the promised new king that God had said he would send. Then one day they heard a man called John shouting out, 'Get the road ready for the Lord! Make a straight path for him. Fill up every valley and level every mountain and hill. Straighten the crooked paths and smooth out the rough roads. Then everyone will see the saving power of God' (Luke 3:4–6).

What a strange thing to say! But the people were intrigued by John and flocked into the desert to listen to what he had to say. Some thought John was the Messiah, the promised new king, but John was very quick to put them right and told the people that he wasn't even good enough to untie the new king's sandals.

Like the prophets before him, John told the people to turn from the things they were doing wrong as a way of getting ready to meet the Messiah. As a sign that they were serious about putting things right, John invited the people to be baptized right there in the River Jordan. The prophets before John had used other picture images to show the people how they needed to change on the inside those things that they knew were wrong. We call it being 'purified' or 'made pure'.

Talk with the children about what images we could use to show the meaning of 'being purified'. Now read Malachi 3:1–4 for some more clues.

REFLECTION

Light the Advent candles for weeks 1 and 2 and play some quiet music. Remind the children that Advent is the time when we get ready to celebrate the birthday of Jesus. Invite the children to think about what they might do to get ready to wish him happy birthday.

PRAYER

Dear Lord Jesus, thank you that you came down to earth to show us how to live with one another. This Christmas, help us to get ready to welcome you again in our hearts and in our actions. Amen

SONGS

Go tell it on the mountain
Colours of day

FOLLOW-ON WORK

Look in Luke 1:5–21 and Luke 1:39–45 to find out a bit more about who John was and how John and Jesus were both very special babies. Talk about promises and what it means to keep a promise. Talk together about how God kept his promise to the people of Israel when he sent Jesus to be their new king.

✳

ADVENT 3: BE JOYFUL

ZEPHANIAH 3:14–20; LUKE 3:7–18

INTRODUCTION

This assembly will continue the story of how John told the people to get ready to meet Jesus by being joyful in the way they give to one another.

FOCUS

The focus is a low table covered with a purple cloth. In the centre of the table place the Advent wreath, but before the children arrive exchange one of the four purple candles for a pink candle.

Welcome the children and ask them if they notice anything different about the focus table. When they mention the pink candle, explain that the third Sunday of Advent is often called 'Gaudete Sunday' and that the word *gaudete* means 'rejoice' or 'be happy'. The pink candle reminds us that today we rejoice as we look forward to celebrating the birthday of Jesus.

Songs

Sing a song of joy at this point—for example, 'Give me joy in my heart, keep me praising' or 'Rejoice in the Lord always'.

Remind the children how, in last week's assembly, they heard how John the Baptist had told the people that they needed to get ready to welcome Jesus the Messiah, their new king. Many of the people who listened to John were baptized in the River Jordan, but others asked John again what they had to do.

Invite the children to listen to the reading from Luke 3:10–14 to see if it gives any clues about what John said. (You might involve some children in acting this bit of the story.)

Christmas is a time when we give and receive presents. Ask the children which they like best—giving or receiving. Talk about gifts that cost money, and gifts of the heart that money can't buy. John wanted the people to give generously, to share all that they had. He told the people not to take more than was rightfully theirs and not to cheat others. Ask the children what they think John would have said to us today.

REFLECTION

Light the first three candles on the Advent wreath (including the pink candle). Place a globe in front of the focus table or hold up a map of the world or project it on to an overhead projector. Invite the children to think about those places in the world where people don't have enough to eat… where there isn't enough money for simple medicines that could make children better… where there is no clear running water. Remind the children that there are enough resources in our world for everyone to have what they need, but even in our own towns and cities people go hungry.

Think about all the presents, special food and parties that people will enjoy this Christmas, and remember that for many people Christmas will be just like any other day, with no special food or presents.

PRAYER

Dear Lord Jesus, help us to share with those around us who don't have as much as we have. Help us to remember this Christmas the children in the world who are hungry and unwell and who need our help. Amen

FOLLOW-ON WORK

The school may have been involved in encouraging the children to bring a gift in a shoebox for children in other parts of the world. This week might be a good week to gather these gifts or to talk about them and the parts of the world to which they are being sent.

Think together about other ways, as a school, the children might share what they have with one another or others in the community. This might include inviting older people in the community, or in local nursing homes, to a school carol service or nativity play. Encourage the children to look out for Fair Trade goods in the supermarket. Talk about how these foods help people in different parts of the world to get a fair wage for their goods.

✱

ADVENT 4: A SONG OF PRAISE

LUKE 1:39–55

INTRODUCTION

This final assembly of Advent focuses on Mary's song of praise at the news that she is going to be the mother of God's son.

FOCUS

The focus is a low table covered with a purple cloth. In the centre of the table, place the Advent wreath and a scroll. The scroll should look old and important. It could be tied with a red ribbon. When unrolled, it will show four symbols from the four weeks of Advent and a simple nativity scene. You will find templates for the symbols on pages 107–109. The symbols will be:

- Stars for Advent 1. (We need to watch for the signs of Jesus coming.)
- Crown for Advent 2. (The prophets told the people to get ready for a new king.)
- Pink candle for Advent 3. (John told the people to be joyful in their giving to others.)
- Mary for Advent 4. (Mary sings a song of praise to God.)

Welcome the children and tell them that this is the last week of Advent and that it is nearly time to celebrate the birthday of Jesus. Look at the focus table and pick up the scroll. Wonder about the scroll—how old and important it looks. Explain to the children that scrolls often had important messages written on them. Ask the children if they know what this scroll could be about. Invite two children to come and hold one end of the scroll while you unroll it.

Slowly unroll the scroll one section at a time. Pause at each section to recap on the messages of the three previous weeks of Advent.

Unroll the fourth section of the scroll to reveal a simple outline of Mary. Remind the children of Mary's story—how she was a young teenager who lived in Nazareth and was engaged to Joseph a carpenter in the village, and how one day an angel came to Mary with a very special message. The angel told Mary that she was going to have a baby and was to call him Jesus. The angel went on to say that Jesus would be the promised new king that the prophets had talked about—that he was the Messiah, God's very own son. Mary was very surprised by what the angel said.

Then the angel told Mary that her relative Elizabeth was also going to have a baby. Mary knew that Elizabeth was elderly and it was believed that she would never have a baby, but Elizabeth's baby was also to have an important part to play in God's very special plan.

When the angel left, Mary set off to visit Elizabeth—even though Elizabeth lived quite a distance away in the hills. When Elizabeth and Mary met, they were very pleased to see each other. The baby inside Elizabeth wriggled with joy and Elizabeth knew straight away that Mary was to have a very special baby. Mary was so happy that she sang a song of praise to God. Today, in some churches, people still sing the song that Mary sang.

Read the first few verses of Mary's song (Luke 1:46–49).

> *Mary said: With all my heart I praise the Lord, and I am glad because of God my Saviour. He cares for me, his humble servant. From now on, all people will say God has blessed me. God All-Powerful has done great things for me, and his name is holy.*

Mary was right, for since that time people have called her 'blessed'. To some people she is simply known as 'the Blessed Virgin Mary'. All over the world, pictures and statues have been painted and made of her. Ask the children if they have seen any paintings or statues of Mary. It might be that the local church or even the school is called St Mary's after her.

REFLECTION

Light four candles on the Advent wreath. Unroll the final part of the scroll to reveal the simple outline of the nativity scene. Remind the children that everything God promised to the people of Israel came true. Jesus the Messiah, the new king, was born, but not in a palace as some thought he would be.

Light the white candle in the centre of the Advent wreath. Instead, this new king was born in an ordinary stable to ordinary parents, and when he grew up he would turn the world upside down with the wonderful things that he did and amazing things he had to say.

PRAYER

Father God, we thank you that your promises are true, and that you sent your son Jesus into the world. Thank you that we can celebrate his birthday this Christmas.

SONGS

Favourite Christmas carols

FOLLOW-ON WORK

Look at paintings of Mary. You may find some on Christmas cards. Let the children paint their own pictures of Mary or make models out of clay. Look at Mary's song of praise and then invite the children to write their own songs of praise to God.

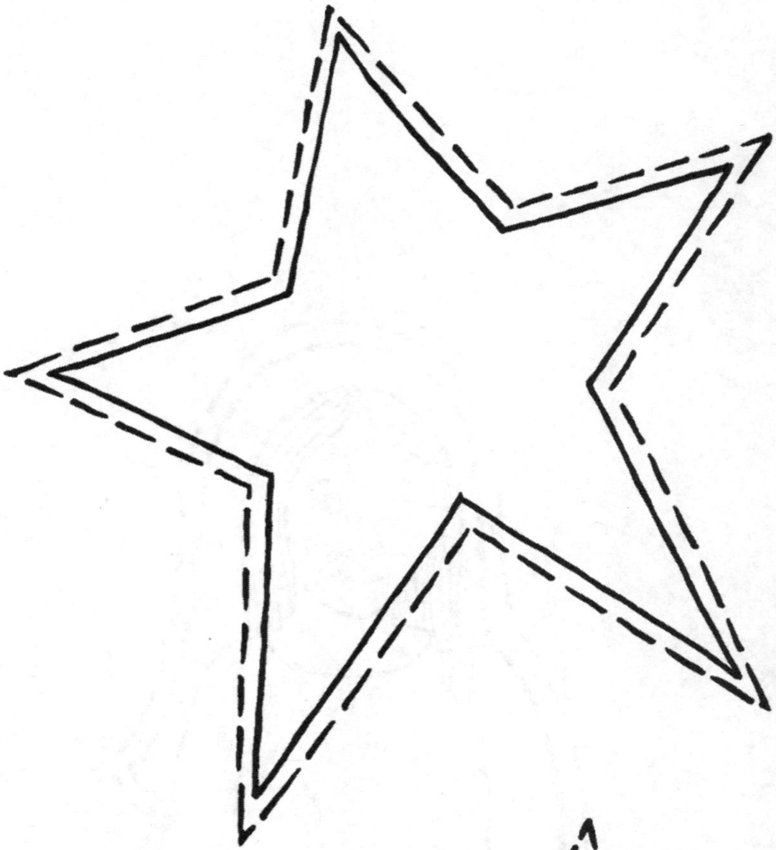

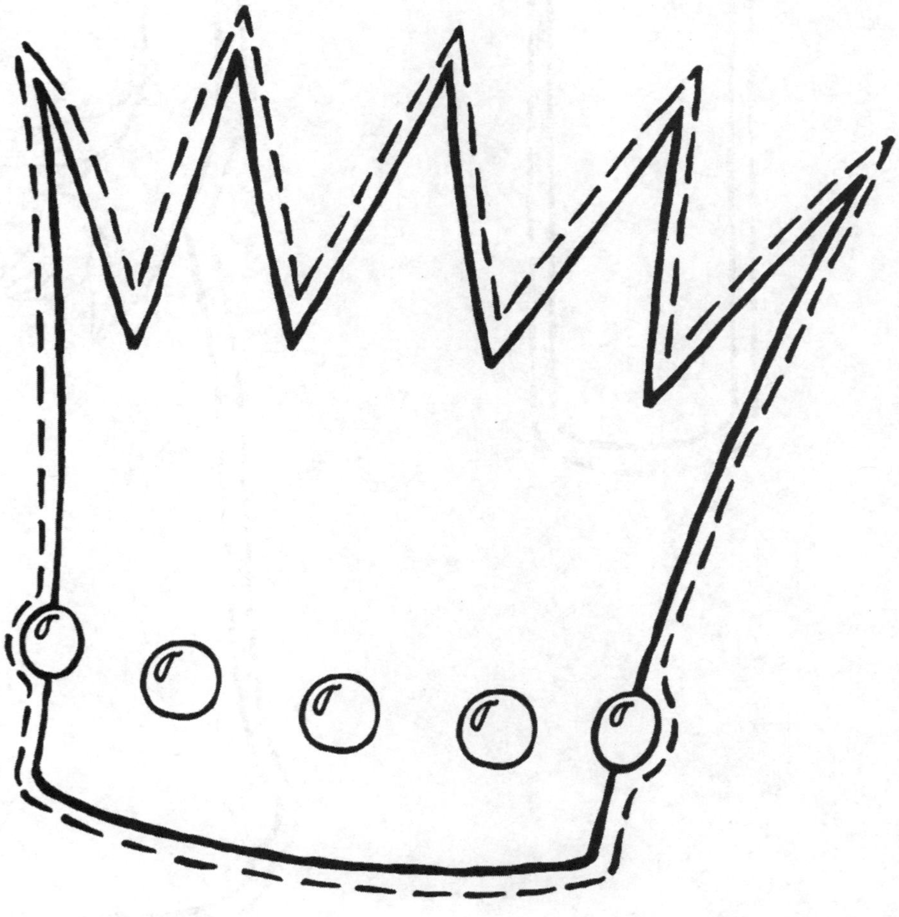

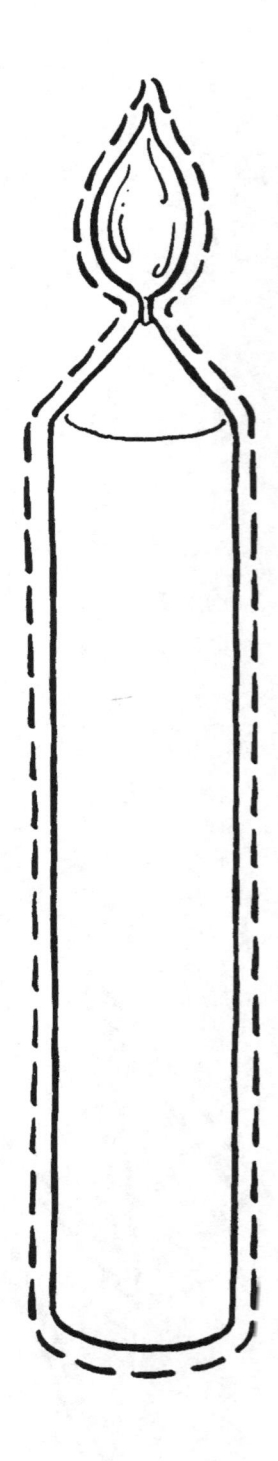

Reproduced with permission from *Sharing Life Through Advent* published by BRF 2004 (1 84101 306 4)

109 Reproduced with permission from *Sharing Life Through Advent* published by BRF 2004 (1 84101 306 4)

OTHER RESOURCES FROM BARNABAS

Visit www.brf.org.uk for information about Barnabas

The Gifts of Baptism

An essential guide for parents, sponsors and leaders
MARGARET WITHERS

- Explores eight of the key signs and symbols used in the baptism service.
- A guide for family members and sponsors.
- Clear one-to-one section for adult and child.
- Includes short extracts from the Bible as well as text and prayers from the service.
- Ideal baptism preparation for individuals and as part of a baptism course.

64PP, PB, REF 1 84101 208 4, £4.99

READING LEVEL/APPLICATION
- **Children:** One-to-one resource
- **Church:** Teaching resource for leaders, parents and clergy, gift to give to parents

Following Jesus

JAMES JONES

- A lively and stimulating introduction to the Christian faith.
- Covers the basics of Christian teaching and discipleship as a preparation for confirmation or church membership.
- Accessible format designed to encourage the habit of regular Bible reading and prayer.

64PP, PB, REF 1 84101 203 3, £3.99

READING LEVEL/APPLICATION
- **Children:** Independent reading for 9-11s
- **Church:** Christian basics teaching resource

Welcome to the Lord's Table

MARGARET WITHERS

- Comprehensive teaching manual for all those seeking to welcome children aged 7–10 to participate fully in the eucharist.
- Material suitable both as preparation for receiving the sacrament and as a junior confirmation course.
- Course includes preparation for the leader and ten self-contained units each designed to fit two 40-minute sessions.
- Gives guidance on preparing the congregation, training leaders and involving the family.
- Based on guidelines approved by the House of Bishops.

112PP, PB, REF 1 84101 043 X, £12.99

READING LEVEL/APPLICATION
- **Church:** Teaching resource for 7-10s

Available from your local Christian bookshop or visit the BRF website at **www.brf.org.uk**

BARNABAS RESOURCES INFORMATION

Please keep me informed about new Barnabas services and resources.

Rev/Dr/Mr/Mrs/Miss _____

Address _____

_____ Post Code _____

Telephone _____ Fax _____

E-mail _____

Do you have responsibilities in any of the following areas?

Sunday School ☐	Teacher ☐
Children's Club ☐	*Which age group?*
Which age range?	Foundation/Reception ☐
3–5 ☐	KS1 ☐
5–7 ☐	KS2 ☐
7–11 ☐	Educational Adviser/Consultant ☐
8–12 ☐	Church Children's Work Adviser ☐

Other (please specify) _____

Please send me

☐ Annual Barnabas Catalogue

Please send me information about

☐ Seasonal resources
☐ Teaching resources for children
☐ Leadership resources
☐ *Barnabas Live* for schools
☐ Inset training
☐ Training for local church children's leaders
☐ *Bible Unplugged* events for children

☐ I would like to support Barnabas ministry with a donation

Data Protection Notice

Under the new Data Protection Act legislation BRF must obtain your consent to hold and use information about you. Please sign below to confirm your consent.

BRF will use the information supplied above to fulfil your orders, and to service your requests for further information. The information will be stored both electronically on computer and in a manual filing system until you inform us otherwise. It may be used to inform you of other BRF products, activities and services. BRF will not supply your details to any other companies other than to fulfil orders from BRF.

I confirm my consent to the Data Protection Notice above.

Signed: _____

PLEASE RETURN THIS FORM TO: BRF, FREEPOST (OF758), OXFORD, OX2 8YY

Barnabas is an imprint of BRF
Charity No. 233280 / VAT No. GB 238 5574 35

BRF, First Floor, Elsfield Hall, 15–17 Elsfield Way, Oxford OX2 8FG
Tel: 01865 319700 / Fax: 01865 319701 / Email: enquiries@brf.org.uk

Visit the brf website www.brf.org.uk

barnabas

Resourcing children's work in church and school

Simply go to **www.brf.org.uk** and visit the barnabas pages

A Browse our books and buy online in our **bookshop**.

B In the **forum**, join discussions with friends and experts in children's work. Chat through the problems we all face, issues facing children's workers, where-do-I-find…? questions and more.

C **Free** easy-to-use downloadable **ideas** for children's workers and teachers. Ideas include:
  • Getting going with prayer
  • Getting going with drama
  • Getting going with the Bible… and much more!

D In the section on **Godly Play**, you'll find a general introduction and ideas on how to get started with this exciting new approach to Christian education.

E In **The Big Picture**, you'll find short fun reports on Barnabas training events, days we've spent in schools and churches, as well as expertise from our authors, and other useful articles.